the joyful wedding

There shall be heard again
the voice of mirth and the voice of gladness,
the voice of the bridegroom and the voice of the bride,
the voices of those who sing.

—Jeremiah 33:10-11 (RSV)

NICK HODSDON

Nashville   ABINGDON PRESS   New York

Copyright © 1973 by Abingdon Press

All rights reserved.
No part of this book may be reproduced in any manner whatsoever without written permission of the publisher except brief quotations embodied in critical articles or reviews. For information address Abingdon Press, Nashville, Tennessee.

Library of Congress Cataloging in Publication Data

HODSDON, NICK, 1941-
　　The joyful wedding.
　　1. Marriage service. I. Title.
BV199.M3H6　　265'.5　　73-8421

ISBN 0-687-20651-0

Scripture quotations noted RSV are from the Revised Standard Version of the Bible, copyrighted 1946, 1952, 1971 by the Division of Christian Education, National Council of Churches, and are used by permission.

Scripture quotations noted NEB are from the New English Bible, copyright © the Delegates of the Oxford University Press and the Syndics of the Cambridge University Press, 1961, 1970.

Scripture quotations noted Phillips are reprinted with permission of Macmillan Publishing Co., Inc. from *The New Testament in Modern English*, 1958, 1960, 1972 by J. B. Phillips.

Scripture quotations noted JB are from *The Jerusalem Bible*, copyright © 1966 by Darton, Longman & Todd, Ltd. and Doubleday & Company, Inc.

Scripture quotations noted TEV are from the Today's English Version of the New Testament. Copyright © American Bible Society 1966.

MANUFACTURED BY THE PARTHENON PRESS AT
NASHVILLE, TENNESSEE, UNITED STATES OF AMERICA

Raison d'être

(We called it that because nobody would read it if we called it "Foreword")

Weddings should be engaging and moving and fun. But too often, those to whom the wedding is most important are distracted by tension and anxiety and worry and just plain fatigue, and may not be able to appreciate what's happening. The elements of the service (and especially the musical elements) sometimes follow a tradition of their own, isolated and insulated as "Wedding Manners" or "Wedding Music." They can be woefully irrelevant to the lives in the gathered community, and they can turn a joyful occasion into something sepulchral and somber.

We find that the ease and the gentleness and the spontaneity of the folk music idiom help the wedding couple and their friends and families to relax and enjoy what should be one of the most memorable and enjoyable events in their lives. And we feel that the bride and groom should be the key people in the planning and the leading of the service. It is the aim of this book to help them reflect, beforehand and during the service, on what their wedding is really all about.

The music in this book was designed for easy congregational singing. The rest of the book is designed to show you how to use the music and its idiom. The resulting services can be done with one guitar and one sure voice, or they can happily encompass the contributions of all the guitars, banjos, and bass fiddles in the family, plus any stray flutes, tambourines, bongos, or cowbells available, and all the singers who'd like to help. A few really terrible voices among the leaders can help a congregation to feel that they have nothing to lose by turning loose and singing out. A few good harmonizing voices can support the congregation, and the results can really be beautiful. The congregation usually needs only the printed words—the persuasiveness of the guitars and the informal friendliness of the singers and worship leaders will do the rest.

Singing, even when you sing the wrong notes, is somehow so "right." So relax and let good things happen!

Contents

The Elements of the Traditional
  Wedding Service 7
Sundry Suggestions 9

I. Ideas for Planning Wedding Celebrations

The Whole Event 11
  Significance
  Outside Environment
  Inside Environment
  Flowers
  Clothing
  Mood
  Content

The Marriage Rite 16
  Processional
  Greeting, Preparation, and Charge
    to the Couple
  Readings
  Meditations or Sermon
  Leave-taking
  Introduction to the Vows
  Promises and Vows
  Blessing and Giving of Rings
  Ceremony of the Sweet and
    Bitter Wines
  Affirmation and Pronouncement
  Nuptial Blessings
  The Lord's Prayer
  Kiss of Peace
  Benediction
  Recessional
  Confession and Assurance of Pardon

The Service of Holy Communion 29
  Why Have Communion at a
    Wedding?
  The Meanings of Communion
  Offertory
  The Communion Rite
  Holy Communion and the
    Agape Feast
  Outline of the Complete Nuptial Mass

II. Scriptural References Which Could Be Used at Weddings 37
  Call to Worship
  Bridal Procession
  Entrance of the Bride and Groom
  Reflections on Creation
  Praise of the Groom
  Praise of the Bride
  Praise of the Congregation
  Praise of the Institution of Marriage
  Preparation for Leave-taking
  Tender Expression of Love
  Meditations on Love and Marriage
  For an Agape Feast
  For Holy Communion
  Vows and Statements of Commitment
  Affirmation
  Recessional
  A Note on the Song of Solomon
  Other Songs from the Secular
    Sphere That Could Be Used at
    Weddings

III. New Music for Weddings

  A Song for the Processional
    "Joy Is Now" 44
  Reflections, in Music, on Love,
    Marriage, and Friendship
    "Man Is the Joy of Man" 46
    "Love Is a Double Helix" 48

THE JOYFUL WEDDING

For Preparation, Readings and Meditations, Leave-taking, Vows, Rings
  "Into Living" 50
  "The Raddle of Love" 52
  "Unfolding" 55
  "Go Watch a Bird" 57
For Silent Prayer, Confession and Absolution
  "Father Almighty" 59
For Gathering Together at the Offertory
  "May That Circle Be Unbroken" ... 60
For the Greeting of Peace
  "Pax Vobiscum" 61
For Gathering, Parting, and Communion
  "There's Many a River" 62

For the Liturgy of the Lord's Supper
  The Canon of the Mass 64
  The Lord's Prayer 66
  Sanctus and Benedictus 68
  Memorial Acclamation 70
  The Great Amen 71
For the Recessional
  "On My Journey" 72

IV. One Version of How This Could All Fit Together

Planning List for Designing Your Wedding 75

Final Checklist 78

The Elements of the Traditional Wedding Service

(In official jargon, "The Form of Solemnization of Matrimony")

The traditional prayer books and service books of the Episcopal, Lutheran, Presbyterian, Methodist, United Church of Christ, and Roman Catholic churches follow the same basic patterns for weddings. The Lutherans add authoritative quotations from God, Jesus, Paul, and Peter; the Baptists and Disciples of Christ generally omit the formal invitation and the formal prayers. Here is the basic outline of the traditional service of matrimony:

Greeting and Preparation (Dearly beloved, we are gathered . . .)
Charge to the Couple (I require and charge you both . . .)
Promises (Wilt thou have this woman/man . . .)
Leavetaking (Who giveth this woman . . .)
Vows (I ———— take thee ———— . . .)
Blessing of the Rings (Bless, O Lord, this ring . . .)
Giving and Receiving of Rings (With this ring I thee wed . . .)
Affirmation (O God, who has so consecrated . . .)
    (Those whom God has joined . . .)
Pronouncement (Forasmuch as ———— and ———— have consented . . .)
Nuptial Blessings (Various)
Lord's Prayer
Benediction (Selected)

For Roman Catholic nuptial services the complete texts of the most recently revised rites for celebrating marriage during Mass and outside of Mass can be found in a little book called *Together for Life,* published by Ave Maria Press.

As a guide to the content of a marriage service in traditional language, the Order for the Service of Marriage as it appears in the current *Book of Worship for Church and Home* of The United Methodist Church is good.

As an example of a standard denominational wedding service in more contemporary language, I recommend the new (1970) Presbyterian wedding service. This is the finest new denominational service of matrimony I've seen so far; it's quite surprising to find something so graceful to have been written by a committee!

All the major denominations have adopted or are provisionally considering contemporary versions of the marriage rite. Ask your minister for copies of both the traditional and revised services of your denomination, for comparison. You might want to use some parts of each.

THE JOYFUL WEDDING

What wor-ries has a but-ter-fly?

A Note on Idealism

Yes, most of the songs in this book are idealistic and romantic. But if you can't be romantic on your wedding day, when can you be, for heaven's sake? By way of balance, see "Into Living," p. 50, and "On My Journey," p. 72: "On our pilgrim journey, through the storms, through the sea; Trials and tribulations still that none can foresee; Joy and tears and laughter, let it come, let it be; I don't want you to weep after me."

This morning I saw a terrible ad in *The New Yorker*. It was an ad for a respectable New York bank that would handle investments for people, and it showed a picture of a man with wrinkled brow reading the financial pages of a newspaper. The lead line of the ad said, "Well, How Much Are You Worth This Morning?" I think that's what the songs in this book are all about—the worth of everybody, every morning.

For birds to earn their right to live is too in-ane for words. They don't put bugs in banks and barns, im-pressing oth-er birds. In-stead they sing

Sundry Suggestions

(gleaned from many a happy wedding)

1. Lots of this isn't going to come out the way you planned it; say a prayer, and stop worrying!

2. In planning the service, a good rule of thumb is to continually alternate music and speech. Refresh every period of spoken word with a period of music, and don't put two pieces of music back to back (except in the warming-up time). Try to select songs that will echo, reinforce, or illuminate the spoken words that precede them.

3. Start the service reflectively; let people get used to the approach; then build in intensity. As people are coming in, have somebody playing and singing some quiet folk songs or spirituals. Then get the congregation to join in on "Kum Ba Yah," or "Michael," or "Jacob's Ladder" and so forth, leading up to more enthusiastic songs like "This Little Light of Mine" or "He's Got the Whole World in His Hands."

4. During this warm-up, sing through a verse or two of the songs you will be using later in the service, so that people can get them into their ears before they come up in the service. Plan for this all to take an extra ten minutes or so (but don't wear the music out). It's especially important to work on the *brief* songs beforehand; if the song has a lot of verses, people will get third and fourth chances to learn it as you're singing it during the service.

5. When the wedding party and the relatives get together beforehand for a rehearsal or a dinner or whatever, begin building the rhythm of the celebration through some scripture reading and some simple shared prayers, and teach them the songs before the wedding. Then they can enjoy it more, and their familiarity will help the rest of the congregation to catch on during the service. This may also win over the mother who has made up her mind to be upset when they don't play "Here Comes the Bride."

6. For that very important post of "song leader," choose somebody warm, friendly, confident, and maybe a little nutty, who can make everybody feel that it's easy to sing along. As each congregational song comes up, have him or her again invite people to sing, telling them where to find it, whether to stand, etc. The song leader will be the essential link between the clergy/wedding party and the guests; be sure that he and the minister know which of them is going to do what in leading the congregation. It is from the song leader that the guests should learn that they are not mere spectators, but that they have come to *do* something with the couple who have invited them.

THE JOYFUL WEDDING

7. The sustaining sound of a flute or clarinet, playing first melody and then harmony lines or descants, can be wonderfully supportive of group singing. It sort of fills in the blanks. In my church we use a xylophone or a set of lyre bells, too, to help pick out the tune and to add embellishments. The clear, ringing sound is quite lovely in hymns sung with guitar accompaniment. Scout around and see what similar resources you can come up with.

8. Give everybody a single outline of the service containing all the words to all the songs and responses that you may want them to join in on, in the order in which they come up in the service. (We've found that if people have the order of worship on one sheet and the words to the songs all together someplace else, most of them just won't fish around to find out where they're supposed to be, and will remain confused and mute.) If space allows, include the words to any solo songs or readings, and the words of the scripture selections, and maybe your vows, too. Here's your chance to identify, acknowledge, and thank readers, singers, ministers, banner makers, flower arrangers. The bride and groom could write a personal message or poem, or could choose an introductory quotation or scripture passage for the first page. (See p. 37.) Ditto or offset or mimeograph these beforehand, and get some of your friends to draw flowers and such on each one with colorful felt tip pens. Make plenty; wedding guests will probably want to keep their copies, and you'll want to send some to friends who couldn't make it.

9. Have somebody up front who can hand copies of the song sheets to the bride and groom, bridesmaids, and ministers, so they can sing along with the congregation.

1. IDEAS FOR PLANNING WEDDING CELEBRATIONS

The Whole Event

None of the stuff on page 7 ("Solemnization of Matrimony") is absolutely necessary. *God didn't ordain it; people just evolved it.* But people came up with it because humankind needs and appreciates symbol and ceremony and ritual. We need to acknowledge the mystical—that there is much that goes beyond even our considerable grasp. Pastors find that people's need for public and religious sanction for their love, and the need for ceremonial confirmation of it, is deeply rooted even among couples who have been living together for some time before deciding on marriage.

A wedding is a ritual which should celebrate, with a variety of rich symbols, the new relationship that has come to exist between two people. The wedding doesn't itself create that new relationship, but it should strengthen and confirm it the way rituals are supposed to do, using signs that convey clearly what we deeply believe but cannot ever fully articulate. It is a rite of passage, the sign of persons moving from one way of life to another. Nobody can move easily from one form of life to another, especially if it implies a lifelong commitment, without symbol and ceremony of the "conversion."[1]

Yet, more and more couples are breaking away from traditional marriage ceremonies, from stylized forms and archaic symbols of the past, in favor of altered or rewritten or newly minted ceremonies that ring more true in the present. The point is this: you *are* free to evolve your own symbols and ceremonies and rituals, if you want to make the ceremony fit you better. Here are some ways to get started.

---
[1] Gabe Huck, ed., *Liturgy* (Journal of the Liturgical Conference), May, 1972, p. 6.

THE JOYFUL WEDDING

Significance

First off, just what should a wedding be—a worship service? a fashion show? a performance? a communal celebration? If a worship service, what's being worshiped—the bride? the Lord? the ceremony itself?

If "surely the Lord's dwelling is with men," maybe the emphasis should be on everybody who has gathered to celebrate the wedding, from which the bride and groom will go to take a new place in this gathering. I think this is the real reason that a wedding takes place not in isolation but in community. What's the significance of inviting a friend to your wedding, if not to have him affirm the marriage and participate in the whole celebration? The insights, the instructions, the covenant of the ceremony may mean as much to someone in the community just now contemplating marriage, or to those married long ago, as they will to the bride and groom.

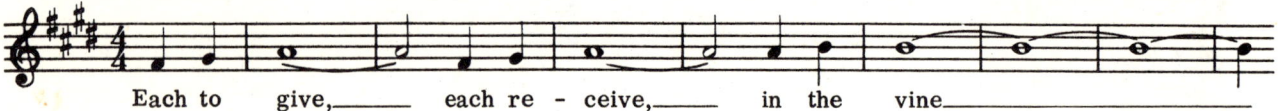

Outside Environment

You can start a feeling of joyful celebration stirring in people while they are still outside the gathering place. Friends could make banners or paper streamers, maybe tied with mirrors or paper flowers, using the wedding colors, to create a festive mood as people approach. Banners could be turned to greet people again when they leave. They could be hung from trees, pillars, standards, or tripods along the walk to the house or church door, along with wind chimes and sprays of flowers.

Inside Environment

Maybe instead of just the usual formal flower arrangements, there should be balloons and colorful banners all around, long festoons of satin ribbon or white crepe paper, and bunches of wild flowers Scotch-taped all over the place.

Balloons are colorful, festive, and very hopeful. Think how bright and buoyant the place would feel if as much thought were given to balloons as is usually given to flowers.

Banners always look great. They somehow manage to be both dignified and festive at the same time, and they're not hard to make, with bright-colored felt and white glue. Tie-dyeing and batiking is even faster for making large banners to be hung in big, high-ceilinged churches, but be sure that the colors complement the dominant colors of the room. For smaller banners you could suggest your favorite symbols or brief quotes.

At the bridal procession, at the recessional, and/or at some particularly buoyant moment of the service, you could give the "flower girl" (or the whole congregation) some commercial bubble solution and let them fill the air with bubbles.

THE WHOLE EVENT

Flowers

Wedding flowers and bridal bouquets needn't be prepared by a commercial florist. Jean Ritchie sings of a girl in Kentucky who goes to the hillside on her wedding morning and breaks off some wild rhododendron for her bouquet. Few florists would come close to that simple loveliness! Some relative will surely have something greening or blooming in the back yard that could be simply tied together with a pretty ribbon. If it's an impossible season, you could get bunches of flowers from a discount flower mart and arrange them yourselves.

Buds o-pen full,_____ and spread their wings,___ and sing the song____ that time is teach-ing.__

Clothing

Wedding clothes are important ceremonially and symbolically. But, like the liturgy, traditional clothing should reflect the real traditions of the real bride and groom, not the sartorial fashions of other people or other generations. Perhaps clothes other than long formal gowns and formal suits would be a more appropriate expression of the real life-style of the bride and groom, for the wedding should take place in real time, rather than in a fashion-show limbo. Contemporary party clothes, long peasant skirts, slacks for everybody, caftans, embroidered Pakistani shirts and blouses—some of these might be more authentic celebration clothes for this wedding.

Close your eyes and picture yourself in clothes that would be ceremonial, and real, and fun, for *you*. What would you wear at a time when you felt good and special and momentous and very, very happy?

The wedding team could make the minister a stole of the same color and material as the bride's or groom's clothing, or a special tie-dyed or hand-batiked one in the wedding colors.

Whether the service is indoors or outdoors, if you want to feel close to the earth at a time when you're being re-rooted so radically, go barefoot and extend this invitation to everybody beforehand.

Shells fall a-way,_____ and roots take hold,___ with arch-ing gold,___ and ten-drils reach-ing;__

13

THE JOYFUL WEDDING

Mood

To get everybody in on the act of celebrating, maybe there should be some happy singing or music-making going on as people come into the church or the living room or the garden or wherever you think the wedding would be happiest. (See Sundry Suggestion #3, p. 9.) Before the music starts, how about playing an "environmental record" of church bells, or of bees buzzing and birds singing? Then the informality of guitar-strumming and folk-style singing can break down any remaining inhibitions and bring a spirit of unity.

If this *is* to be a friendly celebration, it might be good to free people up and dispel the curiously tiptoeing and apologetic feeling that most people insist on bringing as wedding guests. Have the ushers hand everybody a rose or a daisy, or a balloon, or a cluster of grapes or an apple, as he comes in. Or hang a little Indian bell on a length of yarn around the guests' necks, to help them remember that joy is sacred too.

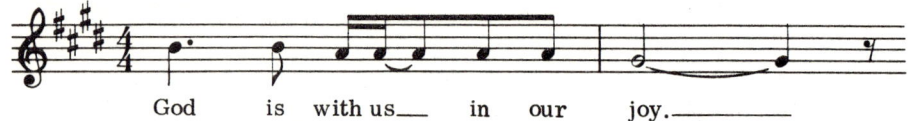

A friend of mine said she hated the idea of the bride's hiding and then appearing before all the eyes and craned necks like a jack-in-the-box, so at her wedding she and the groom greeted the arriving guests and personally took us to our seats. It gave us all a lovely feeling of warmth and friendliness.

No matter who does the welcoming, everyone should be greeted by name, and lone out-of-towners should be introduced to somebody they can sit with. Instead of letting people divide into friends of the bride or friends of the groom, just fill the church or the room from front to back, disregarding sides. Fill up each row before letting anybody into the next one; it'll make the singing and the common feeling so much stronger than it would be with the semi-isolation people tend to inflict on themselves in churches.

A final word: If you once start with a formal atmosphere, then it is very difficult to introduce elements of informality. It usually won't work, and people will feel awkward and confused. But if you start out informally, even playfully, and put all the guests at ease from the start, then quiet moments of great intensity, solemnity, and beauty can grow from their own spirit and authority, as they occur naturally later on in the service, and as they are cued by the particular mood of the songs you choose for them.

Content

Ideally, the bride and groom should write or assemble their own service, saying only what they honestly mean and intend to stick to. Some may prefer a ceremony that doesn't include a pledge to an exclusive or an unbreakable compact, but which simply rejoices in the goodness of their finding and joining each other.

THE WHOLE EVENT

I've seen that when people were committed to owning a house forever, they seemed to settle into it and live in it much more deeply and fully than they ever did in a house they were just renting for the time being, so I think I'd want to say "forever" in my marriage compact; I think it would help me over the inevitable rough spots. However, many may feel that it's *never* realistic to make an eternal promise, "till death us do part," once for all time. Still others may feel that their commitment must be reviewed and renewed from time to time throughout their married lives in order for it to stay alive, and that this commitment to each other need not demand their "forsaking all others."

At a recent ceremony in a commune near Navato, California, the presiding minister of the Universal Life Church pronounced the legal essentials with the words "You're married, as long as you dig it." The things in this book are basically songs of love and interdependence, and are meant to be used for this or *any* kind of communal celebration. But I think every couple needs to be clear about what they're celebrating, and to be realistic and bone-honest about the content of their pledges and intentions.

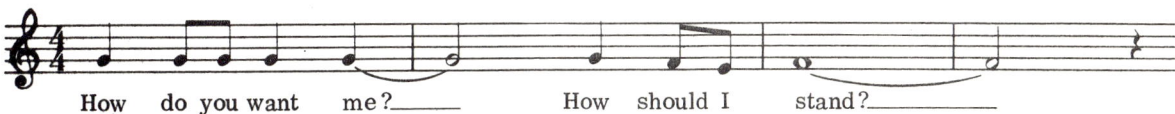

The Marriage Rite

Processional (Song: "Joy Is Now," p. 44)

Whatever the actual terms of commitment chosen, the celebration at which two people proclaim to the world that they're glad they found each other is bound to be a happy one. The processional itself could set the mood of liveliness and joy. For a call to worship, you could have the minister and/or others with good voices read Jeremiah 33:10b-11: "There shall be heard again the voice of mirth and the voice of gladness, the voice of the bridegroom and the voice of the bride, the voices of those who sing!" (RSV); and Psalm 68:24-26: "Thy solemn processions are seen, O God, the processions of my God, my King, into the sanctuary—the singers in front, the minstrels last, between them maidens playing timbrels: 'Bless God in the great congregation, the Lord, O you who are of Israel's fountain!'" (RSV); and, most exuberant, Psalm 57:7b-9: "I will sing and make melody! Awake, my soul! Awake, O harp and lyre! I will awake the dawn! I will give thanks to thee, O Lord, among the peoples; I will sing praises to thee among the nations." (RSV) (Perhaps the song leader ought to read that one.)

The groom and the bride could read this exchange from the Song of Solomon 8:13-14—

Groom: O you who dwell in the gardens, my companions are listening for your voice; let me hear it.
Bride: Make haste, my beloved, and be like a gazelle or a young stag upon the mountains of spices. (RSV)

Then you could have the bride, with her family and her bridesmaids, and the groom, with his family and his groomsmen, process together down parallel aisles from separate doors at the back of the church, to meet finally at the altar, while everybody is singing "Joy Is Now." Just be sure that somebody is committed to keeping the music going in case the congregation stops singing while watching the procession!

16

THE MARRIAGE RITE

Greeting, Preparation, and Charge to the Couple *(Song: "The Raddle of Love," p. 52; "Unfolding," p. 55; "There's Many a River," p. 62)*

In the traditional service, the Greeting and Preparation just told everybody that they were, indeed, dearly beloved; and then simply said what the church thought a marriage covenant was all about. Those who prefer the more traditional structure may wish seriously to work through their covenant, and help the congregation understand it better, by rewriting the words that appear in their own prayer book or service book. Just straightening out the sentence order and putting everyday words in the place of obsolete or unclear phrases can make old verities ring again. (For instance, "in the presence of these witnesses" could become "before this community." "If any man can show just cause why they may not be lawfully joined together, let him now speak, or else hereafter forever hold his peace" could become "If anyone knows a reason why they shouldn't be legally married, he should tell us now, or leave them in peace forever.")

Ann Grant and Phil West rewrote the Greeting, Preparation, and Charge this way:

> *Minister:* Brothers and sisters in Christ, we have gathered before God to join this man and this woman in marriage. We remember that our vows to each other in marriage are like our vows to God in the church. They are not to be taken lightly, but with honest searching and humble prayer. These two persons come now to be joined in God's service. If anyone has a good reason why they should not be joined here, let him speak now or hold his peace.
>
> *People:* As you have asked your sharpest questions and have revealed your deepest secrets to God in private, we now ask you to declare your promises to God and before all of us. We believe that if you hold to what you declare, God will bless your marriage with joy and will build your home in peace.

Maybe instead of just inviting somebody to say why they "should not be joined here," somebody could say why they *should* be joined. Some excellent reasons can be found in Ecclesiastes 4:7-12. It's not too soon to be doing some more music; "The Raddle of Love" might work well here, with or without the scripture on which it was built.

Readings *(Songs: See below.)*

In a complete nuptial Mass or Eucharist, there will be scripture readings later during the Liturgy of the Word (see p. 35). If the wedding is not part of a Communion service, or if the Liturgy of the Lord's Supper will be celebrated after the marriage rite without the Liturgy of the Word, the couple may wish to include, at this point, some readings from scripture or from sacred or secular literature that are particularly meaningful to them. These should be illuminated with songs of course. Suggestions for both follow. The readings could be done by the couple, by family, by friends, from their seats in the room or from different areas in the church. A glorious, if bewildering, assortment of scripture readings can be found on pages 37-42. Of all of these, I favor:

Ruth 1:16-17 (p. 42), followed by the song "Into Living" (p. 50).

Or a selection of verses from the Song of Solomon (p. 38), followed by the song "Man Is the Joy of Man" (p. 46).

THE JOYFUL WEDDING

Or Genesis 2:4b-7, 18-24, then Genesis 1:26-31a (pp. 37-38), followed by verses one and two, with refrains, of "Love Is a Double Helix" (p. 48); then Matthew 19:4-6, followed by the last verse, refrain, and coda of "Helix."

Or Matthew 6:25-34, followed by "Go Watch a Bird" (p. 57).

In addition, the bride and groom will surely have some other favorite scriptures or some inspirational readings on love, marriage, and life together (from Gibran, Teilhard, etc.) to consider as well.

But if you haven't considered it elsewhere, please consider my very favorite passage: Ecclesiastes 4:7-12 (p. 39), followed by "The Raddle of Love" (p. 52).

Meditations or Sermon *(Songs: anything from p. 44 to p. 58!)*

Instead of or in addition to a thoughtful speech given by a minister or family friend, you could have someone preach a sermon by dancing it, or writing a meditation song for you and singing it. Have friends or family give a homily through a film presentation—slides, or home movies with recorded music and a narration; or excerpts from commercially prepared motion pictures.

Ask an older couple (your parents?) who have been married for decades to talk about marriage and what they've seen and found; ask a recently married couple to talk about the period of adjustment; have a time for extempore words of wisdom from anybody in the gathered community. There's a well of helpful experience before you!

Leave-Taking *(Songs: "Unfolding," p. 55; "Love Is a Double Helix," p. 48; "On My Journey," p. 72)*

Many societies have recognized that the marriage ritual is not only for the bride and groom, but that in a very real sense the bride's whole family is marrying the groom's whole family, and the rite of passage must reflect the rather stupendous nature of this event, which will change so many lives. Hence the dowries, the bride-prices, the days of preparation, the concern and involvement of so many relatives.

This still holds true in our culture, more than the bride and groom may recognize. And since a newly married couple in our society typically wants to set up an independent home instead of joining the household of the bride or of the groom, the inclusion of a "leave-taking" ceremony makes great sense. (It might be ritually even more important if the newly wed couple will be living with the parents for awhile.)

In leave-taking, both generations can acknowledge their appreciation of what they have given

THE MARRIAGE RITE

to each other, and can also acknowledge their mature independence from each other. This could include grandmothers, too; it could give the parents a more active part in this celebration which may affect them so much; and it could be more meaningful than the traditional "giving the bride away."

A little snippet of leave-taking traditionally occurs between the Promises and the Vows. To quote from "The Form of Solemnization of Matrimony" according to the Book of Common Prayer of the Episcopal Church: "Then shall the Minister say, 'Who giveth this Woman to be married to this Man?' The father of the Woman, or whoever gives her in marriage, shall answer 'I do.' Then shall they give their troth to each other in this manner. The Minister, receiving the Woman at her father's or friend's hands, shall cause the Man with his right hand to take the Woman by her right hand, and to say after him as followeth. . ."

Have you ever wondered what this was all about? Here the father ritually gives his daughter to the church, which then passes her on to her new master. Why not give the groom away, too? And isn't the mother just as much involved as the father?

Perhaps before the words of leave-taking there could be a simple circle dance (or even a "circle walk") with a soloist singing a quiet song such as "Shalom Havarim," or "Unfolding" (p. 55), or the refrain of "Love Is a Double Helix" (p. 48), or a slower version of "On My Journey" (p. 72). The immediate family of the bride and groom could hold hands, moving in a ring to symbolize the merging of the two families and the new, united relationship of which all the members should be aware. After the circle dance, the bride and groom could walk away from the circle together. "Therefore a man leaves his father and his mother and cleaves to his wife, and they become one flesh" (Genesis 2:24 RSV).

When I'm on my jour-ney, don't you weep af-ter me;

Nan Langdon and Scott Steketee wrote the following leave-taking ceremony for their wedding:

Minister: We have heard that he who made them from the beginning made them male and female, and said, "For this reason a man shall leave his father and mother and be joined to his wife, and the two shall become one." With deep gratitude, Scott and Nan now leave their parents and turn to each other.

Groom: Thank you more than I can say for giving me life and caring for me, for sustaining me and helping me to develop in my own way. As I leave you to join Nan and begin a new family, I give you these flowers as a sign of my love.

Groom's Father: Scott, Doris and I could spend an hour enumerating all the things we wish for you in your coming life together. We do not wish you a life of ease and comfort but rather the ability to stand up under difficulties and challenge.

Bride: (She also gives flowers to her father and mother, using the same words.)

Bride's Father: Nan, you must know that you go with your mother's and my love, our blessings, and the devout wish that your and Scott's life together will be useful, happy, and satisfying.

THE JOYFUL WEDDING

The bride may want to use different words from the groom in her leave-taking, and the couple might address themselves to their whole families rather than to just the mothers and fathers. (Picture the couple surrounded by laughing and crying and beaming relatives!)

Appropriate scripture quotations for leave-taking can be found on p. 39. And what a perfect time to sing "Sunrise, Sunset" from *Fiddler on the Roof!*

The hard, joy-ous ven-ture of liv-ing to-geth-er

Introduction to the Vows

The old and the new can be used together—if it's planned sensitively without dragging the congregation over the cobblestones of stylistic change. The bride in many a commune has worn her grandmother's wedding dress. A strong and beloved hymn such as "Amazing Grace" can be used along with something like "Love Is a Double Helix," and a vernacular rendering of the Charge to the Couple could be used along with the venerable tone of this Introduction to the Vows from the Westminster Confession of Faith, if the bride and groom like the way they flow together:

"Christian marriage is an institution ordained of God, blessed by our Lord Jesus Christ, established and sanctified for the happiness and welfare of mankind, into which spiritual and physical union one man and one woman enter, cherishing a mutual esteem and love, bearing with each other's infirmities and weaknesses, comforting each other in trouble, providing in honesty and industry for each other and for their household, praying for each other, and living together the length of their days as heirs of the grace of life." (Westminster Confession of Faith, 1643.)

But bonds grow strong,___ and love un-folds,___ and har-vests gold___

Promises and Vows (Songs: "Man Is the Joy of Man," p. 46; "Love Is a Double Helix," p. 48; "Into Living," p. 50; "The Raddle of Love," p. 52.)

The Promises and the Vows are just about the same thing. Traditionally the minister puts the Promises to the couple in the form of questions, to which they answer "I do" or "I will." Then the bride and groom say the Vows to each other. The two forms could easily be combined.

Many people consider the Promises and Vows to be the girders of the covenant, so the couple really should compose their own to be sure of just what they want to pledge to each other. The preface to the new Lutheran marriage service (1972) states: "The promises are the bride's and groom's own, and provision should be made for those who want to write their own form of the promises. . . . For it is not a formula, but the promises of fidelity that makes a marriage." In the new Lutheran service, the minister says to the couple, "N. and N., if it is your intention to share with each other your laughter and your tears and all that the years will bring, by your promises bind yourselves now to each other as husband and wife."

THE MARRIAGE RITE

Dottie Bass and Jim Fraser wrote the following vows for their wedding:

> In the presence of God and our friends I declare my love for you.
> I affirm our covenant to live together, to struggle together,
> to share all things together,
> in times of joy and in times of pain.
> I promise to bear with you in strength and in weakness
> and to pray with you in all seasons, depending always on God's grace.

In my weak-ness, in my strength, with my arm out to love you____

In the Episcopal *Book of Common Prayer,* the woman says "I *give* thee my troth," whereas the man says, "I *plight* thee my troth." The woman *gives* her promise of fidelity, whereas the man only has to *indicate his intention* to be faithful. Anybody who notices this vestige of male chauvinism would probably want to alter it. Still, the bride's vows don't have to be the same as the groom's; they are different people, and will support each other in different ways. Nan Langdon and Scott Steketee began their vows this way:

> S: I promise, Nan, to help you, through patient encouragement, in expressing both your feelings and your ideas.
> N: I promise, Scott, to work with you in becoming more sensitive to other people's feelings, wants, and needs.
> S: I promise, Nan, to help you live life today in full enjoyment of the moment, without concern or worry over what tomorrow may bring.
> N: I promise, Scott, to help you see long-term aspects of situations and to plan ahead with you for the future.

To - mor-row's fields_ are bare if you don't sing._____

Peggy Webber and Al Scott didn't intend to vary the words with which they stated their simple, moving, concise, very beautfiul vows to each other, but they came out a little differently. Peggy got hers out okay, but when Al started saying his, Peggy began crying and laughing, which made lots of other people start crying and laughing, so it took Al a good while longer to get through. Here's how theirs went:

> Peggy, I love you and I need your love.
> I trust you, and I trust our love.
> Because of our love, I am making a commitment to you about
>   the future.
> Peggy, I want you to be my wife and I want to be your husband.
> I affirm my commitment to you before our families and friends
>   here today.

THE JOYFUL WEDDING

> I promise to support you in who you are and in the ways you
>   are growing,
> To be there for you in times of fear, confusion, and difficulty,
>   in growth, joy, and fulfillment,
> So that our love will continue to grow and expand to those
>   around us.
> Peggy, wear this ring as a symbol of my love and my promise.

So love must ex-pand, to vi-brate in oth-ers

In the Presbyterian service of marriage in contemporary language, the vows appear as:

> _____, I promise with God's help to be your faithful husband, to love and to serve you as Christ commands, as long as we both shall live.
> I give you this ring as a sign of my promise.

But the old traditional Presbyterian vow is still very beautiful:

> I, _____, take thee, _____, to be my wedded wife; and I do promise and covenant, before God and these witnesses, to be thy loving and faithful husband; in plenty and in want; in joy and in sorrow; in sickness and in health; as long as we both shall live.
> This ring I give thee, in token and pledge, of our constant faith, and abiding love.

You may want to take your vows entirely from scripture, or from secular literature. There are some wonderful exchanges in the Song of Solomon which would be marvelous, if a little intoxicating, for the bride and groom to read to each other at this point. You'll find some of them on pages 38-39, 42.

Ruth's words to Naomi (Ruth 1:16-17) speak beautifully of a covenant of love and loyalty: "Entreat me not to leave thee, or to return from following after thee: for whither thou goest, I will go; and where thou lodgest, I will lodge; thy people shall be my people, and thy God my God: Where thou diest, will I die, and there will I be buried: the Lord do so to me, and more also, if aught but death part thee and me" (KJV).

Hosea 2:19 has a more formal tone, in using the marriage covenant as a metaphor for God's loving covenant with his people: "I will betroth you to me for ever; I will betroth you to me in righteousness and in justice, in steadfast love, and in mercy" (RSV).

The bride could read one of these, the groom could read the other, either here before the vows, or as the vows themselves, or earlier at the readings after the Preparation and Charge.

In Erich Segal's *Love Story,* the presiding cleric just says, "Friends, we are here to witness the union of two lives in marriage. Let us listen to the words they have chosen to read on this sacred occasion." The bride used a sonnet by Elizabeth Barrett Browning ("When our two souls stand up erect and strong . . ."), the groom used a section of Walt Whitman's *Song of the Open Road:*

> . . . I give you my hand!
> I give you my love more precious than money,
> I give you myself before preaching or law;

THE MARRIAGE RITE

> Will you give me yourself? will you come travel with me?
> Shall we stick by each other as long as we live?

This would be a good time to sing "Man Is the Joy of Man" or "Into Living" or "Love Is a Double Helix." Or you could sing one song after the groom has stated his vows and another one after the bride has given hers. Or divide a song up and sing one verse after each part.

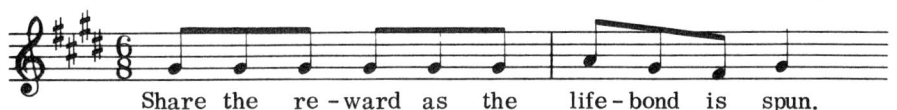
Share the re-ward as the life-bond is spun.

Blessing and Giving of Rings (Songs: "Unfolding," p. 55; "Love Is a Double Helix," p. 48, especially verse 2.)

Many versions of the Promises and Vows incorporate a short ring-giving phrase, almost like an afterthought. But the ring will be the most constant and visible remembrance of the wedding day, and the symbolic quality of the ring can be quite powerful, so it ought not to be passed over so quickly. The more traditional services recognized this; the rings were blessed, were explained, and then the couple made a sort of reiteration of their vows when the ring was given and received, as if the ring symbolically bore the binding force of the vows. The *Form of the Dutch Canon* adds:

> With this ring I wed you;
> With my body I worship you;
> With all that I have I endow you:
> In the name of the Father and of the Son,
> And of the Holy Spirit. Amen.

When Sandy Lloyd's widowed mother remarried at the age of fifty-four, Sandy and I worked out a service that would be appropriate for two older people, both of whom had been married for many years before and who already knew how hard marriage could be. We gave particular thought to the meaning of the rings, and as far as I can remember, we wrote:

> The rings that you now give to each other are like the love that you give to each other:
>
> Your ring is a valuable thing.
> Your ring is a beautiful thing.
> Your ring encircles and embraces, strengthens and holds comfortably, without stifling or squeezing too tightly.
> Your ring is a gift, to be actively given and actively accepted.
> Your ring can be lost or thrown away through carelessness or indifference or inattention.
> But if you value it, your ring will wear well, and won't wear out.
> A ring can go on forever, for a ring has no end.

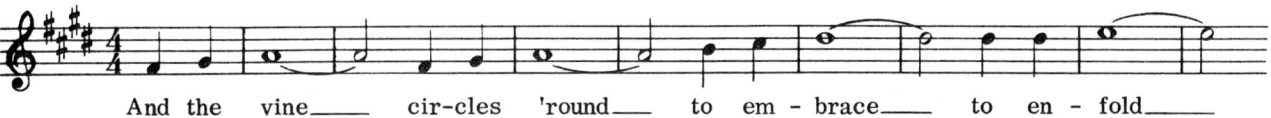
And the vine___ cir-cles 'round___ to em-brace___ to en-fold___

THE JOYFUL WEDDING

Ceremony of the Sweet and Bitter Wines

There's a Quaker tradition in which, at the time of the giving of rings, the bride and groom take sips of sweet and bitter wines, I suppose to signify both the good times and the difficult times that lie ahead as the rings roll unendingly onward. This is the kind of symbol that will really help a wedding to do what rituals are supposed to do, using signs to convey clearly what we deeply believe but cannot ever fully articulate. The minister could articulate it in part by saying something like, "The brimming cups of sweet and bitter wines traditionally symbolize the sweetness and the sadness of the brimful life. Drink together the bitter wine, knowing that anger and frustration will come to challenge your love and union, and to make it grow. Drink together the sweet wine in anticipation of that growth, and of the joy that lies ahead."

Riv - er___ of wine in our lives, cool and burn - ing

Affirmation and Pronouncement (Songs: "There's Many a River," p. 62; "Go Watch a Bird," p. 57; "Man Is the Joy of Man," p. 46.)

These are the minister's traditional words of Pronouncement:

> Forasmuch as _____ and _____ have consented together in holy wedlock, and have witnessed the same before God and this company, and thereto have pledged their faith each to the other, and have declared the same by joining hands and by giving and receiving rings; I pronounce that they are husband and wife together, in the name of the Father, and of the Son, and of the Holy Spirit. Those whom God hath joined together, let not man put asunder. Amen.

But if we believe that marriage is basically a covenant of commitment and sharing, then most couples are married long before they go through the "solemnization of matrimony," so the Pronouncement could be replaced by an acknowledgment or an affirmation of the marriage, said by the whole congregation. This was Jim and Dottie Fraser's acknowledgment:

> *Minister:* As Dorothy and Jim have declared their love and their covenant before us and before God, let us acknowledge and rejoice in their marriage.
> *Congregation:* Jim and Dorothy, we affirm and announce that you are husband and wife, in the name of the Father and of the Son and of the Holy Spirit. Amen!

Even if the bride and groom have been committed to each other for years, this is an exciting moment, no matter who makes the announcement (when Jim and Margie Fitzgibbon were pronounced husband and wife, everybody started to clap!), so during a pre-pronouncement song (maybe a final chorus of "Joy Is Now") you could pass out helium balloons and at the word "Amen" let them all take flight. If the wedding is outside, you could attach wedding announcements made of light paper; you could even release a flight of doves or pigeons! And then sing "Go Watch a Bird." (Seriously, now would be a great time to sing a celebration song, e.g., "Man Is the Joy of Man.") Then everybody could blow whistles or ring bells or gather around to congratulate the bride and groom.

THE MARRIAGE RITE

A scriptural benediction to the Affirmation can be found in Ecclesiastes 9:9—

Enjoy life with the wife whom you love, all the days of your . . . life which he has given you under the sun, because that is your portion in life (RSV).

A wed-ding comes,_ and flows on by,____ and turns to years__

If the wedding is part of a complete nuptial Mass, the service will continue with the Creed or Profession of Faith (see page 35).

If the wedding is simply to be concluded with a celebration of the Lord's Supper, the service will continue with the Nuptial Blessings and the Lord's Prayer (pp. 25, 26), the Confession and Assurance of Pardon (p. 28), the Kiss of Peace (p. 26), and then the Offertory and the rest of the Communion service (p. 31).

If the wedding is not to be part of a service of Holy Communion, the service will now conclude with various Nuptial Blessings, the Lord's Prayer, the Kiss of Peace, a Benediction, and the Recessional. (See below.)

Glo - ry to God, and now give me your hand.

Nuptial Blessings (Songs: "Man Is the Joy of Man," p. 46; "Unfolding," p. 55.)

These prayers are usually said by the presiding minister, but it would be appropriate to have the parents add their blessings, too. Their prayers could be spontaneous, or prepared beforehand if that would make them more comfortable.

In addition to the standard denominational Nuptial Blessings, I particularly like this Blessing of the Marriage at the Eucharist from the Episcopal *Services for Trial Use*:

> Almighty God, in whom we live and move and have our being: Look graciously upon the world which you have made, and on the Church for which your Son gave his life; and especially on all whom you make to be one flesh in holy marriage:
>
> Grant that their lives together may be a sacrament of your love to this broken world, so that unity may overcome estrangement, forgiveness heal guilt, and joy overcome despair. *(Amen.)*
>
> Grant that all married persons who have witnessed this exchange of vows may find their union strengthened and their loyalty confirmed. *(Amen.)*
>
> Grant that the bonds of our common humanity which unite every man to his neighbor, and the living to the dead, may be transformed by your grace, that justice and peace may prevail and your will be done on earth as it is in heaven. *(Amen.)*

Thy King-dom come, thy will_ be done, on earth as it is_ in heav - en.

THE JOYFUL WEDDING

The Lord's Prayer *(See p. 66.)*

There are quite a number of musical settings of this prayer, and many of them aren't really all that musical, or prayerful. I favor the one commonly called "The West Indian Lord's Prayer," or the one gently set (curious as it may seem) to the tune of "Waltzing Mathilda," or the one you'll find on page 66, which (he said modestly) I think is one of the prettiest settings around.

If the Lord's Prayer is rather to be spoken together, it would be very effective to pray it after the Passing of the Peace and the singing of the "Pax Vobiscum."

Kiss of Peace *(Songs: "There's Many a River," p. 62; "Joy Is Now," p. 44; "Pax Vobiscum," p. 61.)*

Before the minister says the benediction, it would be good to have everybody share in the ritual of the Kiss of Peace. This is just a personalization of the common liturgical exchange in which the priest says "Peace be with you" and the congregation all respond with "And with thy spirit." Some worship leader begins "passing the Peace" by taking the hands of someone and saying "Peace be with you, John." John answers, "And also with you, Bill" or "And with your spirit, Bill." He then passes the Peace on to the next person. It's especially nice to speak the name of the person you're greeting, and the physical touching is generally a welcomed sign of unity and reconciliation; I rather like to hug people instead of just taking their hands.

The passing of the Peace will be the couple's very first interaction with the community as man and wife. They could receive the Peace from the minister, or they could initiate it themselves, and then they could go down the center aisle and give the Peace to the first person of each row, who would then pass it down to the others in his row. (Note: People are sometimes slow to catch on to this, even if it's clearly explained beforehand, so you might have to say "Pass it on" to some of them.) If there are several aisles, bridesmaids and groomsmen could help to pass the Peace.

If traffic permits, the musicians could begin a song once the Peace has gotten started ("Joy Is Now" suggests itself; or, most logically, "There's Many a River"), and everybody could circulate

26

THE MARRIAGE RITE

around to exchange the Peace with everybody else, rather like the greetings at the Hymn of Fellowship as now practiced in more and more churches. People who still haven't met could say "Peace" and then introduce themselves, and the Kiss of Peace could give more depth to the old tradition of everybody kissing the bride. This will be far more fun than the tedious and interminable ordeal of the receiving line, and would serve the same purpose.

Here is another thought: it might be symbolically more realistic to have people from the community start the Peace, and then bring it to the bride and groom. At first, family and friends may be supporting, helping, and bringing peace to the newlyweds more than they'll be receiving support, help, and peace from them during the early period of marriage.

At any rate, after everybody has gotten Peaced, you could all sing together the "Pax Vobiscum" found on page 61. It's very simple, and very lovely.

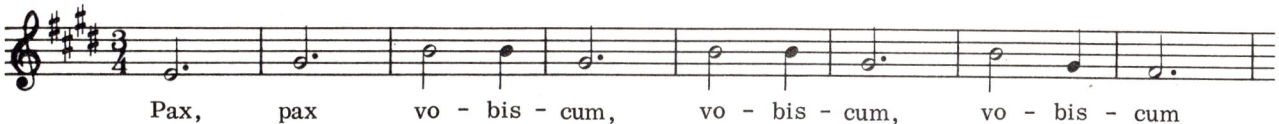

Benediction

For a final Benediction, after the closing prayers (especially if a reception is imminent), the minister could say these lines from Ecclesiastes 9:7—

"Go, eat your bread with enjoyment, and drink your wine with a merry heart, for God has already approved what you do." (RSV)

Then the bride or groom (or both, in turn) could read these marvelous words from the Song of Solomon 7:11-12—

"Come, my beloved, let us go forth into the fields, and lodge in the villages; let us go out early to the vineyards, and see whether the vines have budded, whether the grape blossoms have opened and the pomegranates are in bloom. There I will give you my love." (RSV)

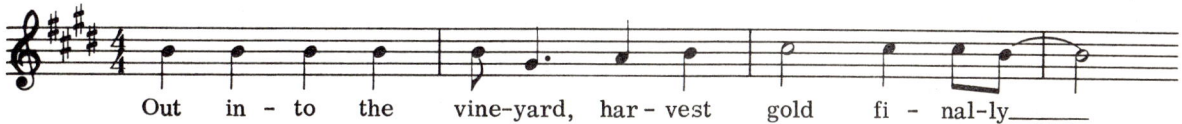

Recessional (Songs: "On My Journey," p. 72; "Joy Is Now," p. 44; "Go Watch a Bird," p. 57.)

Now is the time for the full joy of the day to break out. Now is the time to tap your percussion resources—to pass out things to tap on, things to jingle, things to bang together. Now is the time to coax the congregation into the aisles, to march with the bride and groom on their journey to the next phase of their life together, and to the fellowship that extends the worship service. People could pelt them happily with flowers and blow bubbles over their heads.

When you get outside or into the outer room or hall or whatever, you could gather in a big untidy circle and sing the chorus one final time, and then sing "He's Got the Whole World in His Hands" or "Amen." Or, if the reception is in an adjoining room, just march there all singing.

THE JOYFUL WEDDING

A good recessional song is "On My Journey." But at Al Scott's wedding the guitarist broke into "Yes, Sir, That's My Baby," and somebody joined in with a kazoo. It was beautiful!

Joy and tears and laugh-ter, let it come, let it be!

Confession and Assurance of Pardon (Song: "Father Almighty," p. 59.)

In the ceremony of the sweet and bitter wines, we recognize that man is imperfect and that we are always falling short. It's good to acknowledge these errors and shortcomings, not only to see them so as to try to correct them, but to clear the air; in the words attributed to Peter, to "repent therefore, and turn again, that your sins may be blotted out, that times of refreshing may come from the presence of the Lord" (Acts 3:19 RSV). I like to provide for these "times of refreshing" by including a corporate confession and absolution in *every* worship service, but not all people feel that public confession is wanted. Here is a somewhat heretical call to confession we used at a wedding where some wanted a confession and some didn't:

> All of us sometimes do what we know is wrong, and don't do what we know is right. We can't change until we see what we are doing wrong. We can't help each other until we admit that we all need help. And we can't ask God to help us and forgive us until we admit to him that we need his pardon. Let those of us who feel we need his pardon bring our confession before God now in our prayers.

For a congregational response, we used verses from Psalm 51, followed by silent prayer (so that people could confess or not confess, as they chose):

> Behold, you desire truth in the inward being; therefore teach me wisdom in my secret heart. (51:6 RSV)
> Create in me a clean heart, O God, and put a new and right spirit within me. (51:10 RSV)

You could simply close the silent prayer by singing "Father Almighty," or the minister could say some words of absolution or assurance of pardon. Or, after one verse of "Kum Ba Yah," the congregation could say together the following words, from a service by Phil West:

> As straight as our words have been, God has heard us.
> As deep as our guilt was, he accepts us now.
> As honest as our confession was, we are forgiven.
> As completely as our decision to live Christ's way, we will be given power.
> In the name of Jesus Christ, Amen.

Wash us new, Lord, wash us new.

If you have not celebrated the Kiss of Peace, you might wish to include it here, after the Confession and Assurance of Pardon.

The Service of Holy Communion

Why Have Communion at a Wedding?

It is a Jewish tradition that a wedding hasn't been completed until the bride and groom have shared a meal together, and thus have become a family, doing a particular thing that defines a family. In the Christian tradition, we celebrate this ancient custom together in a very special and wonderful way. The marriage rite, in which a new family unit is instituted in the presence of a continuing family community, is at its fullest and most satisfying when celebrated as part of a service of Holy Communion, also called a Mass or Eucharist.

Like the ancient sacrifice, the dramatic forms of worship are sometimes more important than the words that go with them, because of the importance of feeling and understanding below the level of rational consciousness. It's not because people are hungry that you always have food at a party; the comfortable mystique of eating together is such a vital thing that it makes a gathered company into a sort of family—which is what the community assembled to celebrate the marriage should be anyway.

One couple (Pat Hall and Rand Timmerman) wanted to have a more intimate Communion service, so they had their wedding in two parts. The immediate family and closest friends met for an informal Eucharist in Pat's living room in the morning, where the bride and groom and their parents read the call to worship (which they had written), the scriptures, the offertory, and a meditation on love, as worship leaders along with the priest. Then everybody gathered at the family church in the afternoon along with the complete wedding guest list for a more traditional service of "solemnization of matrimony." We used the same informal folk music styles for both services, and sang one or two of the same wedding songs at both to maintain continuity.

THE JOYFUL WEDDING

The Meanings of Communion

A service of Holy Communion that includes the marriage rite is traditionally called a nuptial Mass or a nuptial Eucharist. Before looking at how to do it, let's look at *why* people do it and what it's all about.

The ancient core of a community worship experience was a sacrifice. *Facio* means "I do"; *sacer* means "a holy thing"; so *sacrifice* just means "to do a holy thing." In the Jewish temple service on which Christian liturgy is founded, an animal was sacrificed as a gift or as an expiation to the god, who might then join the congregation in feasting on the sacrifice, as the vitality of the animal passed into the worshiping community.

There was also a mystical identification of the giver with the gift, so that what happened to the sacrifice happened to the community; as the animal dies, *you* die. The idea was that man must die before God, so that man's true identity could be discovered (just as, in psychotherapy, you die to an old life and something is destroyed every time a new constellation of the personality is created). In a marriage, the partners discard some aspects of their individuality, their independence, etc., to become a new thing, to "become one flesh" (Genesis 2:24). Something dies so that something new can be born.

Live in us, Lord. Help us ev-er live in you, Lord, Live in you.

This sacrifice is now remembered or re-enacted sacramentally. The Christian church saw the sacrifice as fulfilled in Christ (John 6:55-57, etc.), and his offering, dying, and rising is relived in the liturgy. The communicants participate in the awesome thing of putting themselves in the hands of God, to die and rise anew.

In writing about what he called "the Lord's Supper," Paul emphasized the passion and death of Christ, remembering Calvary, emphasizing Christ's atonement for guilt and sin (e.g., "Until the Lord comes, therefore, every time you eat this bread and drink this cup, you are proclaiming his death." [I Corinthians 11:26 JB])

By and large, the Western churches have followed Paul's solemn interpretation of the Lord's Supper as a somber thing. But the Eastern churches have followed a very different tone, that of the earliest Christian communities, who celebrated the breaking of bread (the earliest known Christian act of worship) as a *joyful* rather than as a sorrowful thing. Acts 2:46 says, "Breaking of bread celebrated this in a sort of Messianic banquet. In pre-Christian Jewish apocalypse, one of the

Why were they so happy? They saw that Jesus had brought in a new age, and the breaking of bread celebrated this in a sort of Messianic banquet. In pre-Christian Jewish apocalypse, one of the activities is a first-class dinner, where you will eat the great fish "Leviathan." (Fish came to be the dominant symbol of Christianity.) You will also eat heavenly manna, ground in one of the seven heavens and brought to earth by the Messiah. For the Christians, Jesus *was* the manna (John 6:48-51). Not only that, but they saw that he revealed himself in eating and drinking: "When he was at table with them, he took the bread and blessed and broke it, and gave it to them. And their eyes were opened, and they recognized him" (Luke 24:30-31 RSV); "If one of you hears me calling and opens the door, I will come in to share his meal, side by side with him" (Revelation

THE SERVICE OF HOLY COMMUNION

3:20 JB), etc. The occasion of the Lord's Supper was to remember not the sorrow of his death, but the joy of his resurrection and his presence.

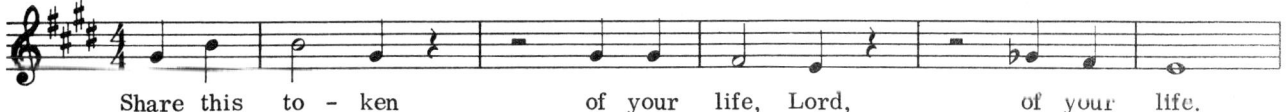
Share this to-ken of your life, Lord, of your life.

Around A.D. 90, people started calling the meal the "Eucharist." This comes from the Greek word *eucharistein,* which means "to give thanks." It was still a full meal, it was joyful, and it was an occasion for thanksgiving. A nuptial Eucharist could be an occasion for giving thanks for the bride, for the groom, for their finding each other, for flowers, for music, for all of us. In the passage from Acts 2:46 quoted above, the Greek authors chose a striking word which means "ecstatic joy." Their Lord's Supper was a happy celebration. With all due respect to Paul, I think it still should be.

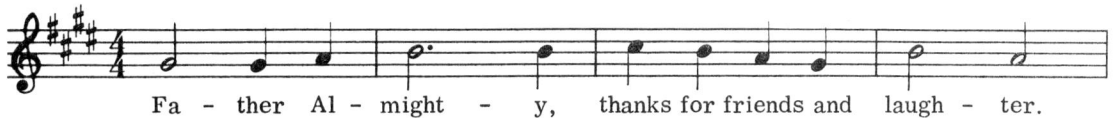
Fa - ther Al - might - y, thanks for friends and laugh - ter.

Offertory

At the Offertory, the bread and wine to be used for Communion, and at the same time the gifts of the people (gifts of money, "alms and oblations," symbolically, the gifts of ourselves), are offered to God for his blessing. If the bride's or groom's family and guests feel a living sense of the supporting influence of the church, it would be appropriate to include a collection of tithes and offerings at this point. Both the gifts of money and the gifts of bread and wine would be symbolically placed before God on the altar or table. One of the Eucharistic prayers of the Roman Catholic Church puts this in very dramatic language: "Almighty God, we pray that your angel may take this sacrifice to your altar in heaven."

Lacking an angel, the bride and groom or some other members of the community could bring the bread and wine to the table. At Pat and Rand Timmerman's wedding, Pat baked the bread herself the night before. And somebody's grandmother may still know how to make homemade wine. During the Offertory at Jim and Margie Fitzgibbon's wedding they brought out platters of cheese and ham, pickles and rye bread, and held what would have been the reception dinner right in the middle of the service, as an agape feast. Then they consecrated some of the bread and wine and continued with a regular service of Holy Communion.

As we gath - er at your ta - ble

If the Offertory were immediately preceded by the Kiss of Peace, the bride and groom would already be at the back of the church or the room and could bring the wine up to the table with them after the "Pax Vobiscum." They could bring the rest of the congregation up with them, too.

THE JOYFUL WEDDING

If the Offertory is a time when we offer ourselves to God, then it would be good to symbolize this by *our* coming to the table along with the other gifts offered. And for people to join together in a supporting group this way would complete the sense of a gathered community in a way that nothing else could. The minister, the song leader, or the bride or groom could ask everybody to come up and be with them for this special meal, even if they chose not to partake of the bread and wine.

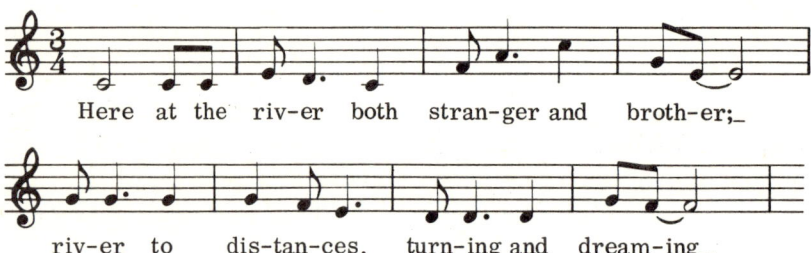

I've been at weddings when as many as three hundred people came up and made a wonderful vibrant circle three or four deep around the Communion table, and the feeling of a real gathered family was incredible. There always seems to be room enough—especially if somebody is on hand to move ornamental chairs or prie-dieus or lecterns out of crowded areas if need be. A good hymn for getting people moving and establishing the sense of communal joy is "May That Circle Be Unbroken" (p. 60). (When inviting the people up, remember to ask them to bring their song sheets.)

Whether everybody gathers at the table or not, this special time of offering gifts to God could provide a chance for people to go beyond the usual limits of material wedding gifts. Just as God gives the bread and wine to us, we can only offer something to God by giving it to other people. ("As you did it to one of the least of these my brethren, you did it to me." [Matthew 25:40 RSV]) In his first epistle, John wrote:

> By this we know love, that he laid down his life for us; and we ought to lay down our lives for the brethren. But if any one has the world's goods and sees his brother in need, yet closes his heart against him, how does God's love abide in him? Let us not love in word or speech, but in deed and in truth. (I John 3:16-18 RSV)

Using this as an offertory sentence, the close friends and relatives of the bride and groom could offer aloud in God's name whatever they could give the couple in terms of continuing love and support in their new life together—an offering of deed rather than just of material gifts. For instance, the parents could offer to give advice when it was wanted, and *not* to give advice when it wasn't. Someone could offer thirty hours of baby-sitting time, should the opportunity occur. A trusted friend could offer himself as paraclete (or "spiritual guide") to the couple, a supporter to the marriage in its growing and binding.

THE SERVICE OF HOLY COMMUNION

The Communion Rite

At the time of the distribution of the elements of Communion, the members of the congregation could break and pass the bread from one to another, and then pass the cup. If the minister prefers, he could break all the bread himself during the Prayer of Consecration and let the bride and groom distribute the bread and wine to the worshipers.

Everyone may already know the folk songs "Kum Ba Yah" or "Let Us Break Bread Together," which could be sung during Communion. But "There's Many a River" (p. 62) is a spell-weaving Communion song that can draw upon the power of so many people gathered and sharing. After the first verse or so, the guitarist could just strum while the words of institution are said over the bread. The next few verses could be sung while the bread is distributed, then there could be another instrumental interlude while the words of institution for the wine are spoken. The song should end with everybody holding hands and feeling the miraculous unity of a close community at worship.

Holy Communion and the Agape Feast

It is the common practice to have a full nuptial Eucharist (in which the marriage rite is a part of the complete Mass) only in the Roman Catholic and Episcopal churches, so an outline of the Episcopal service and the Roman Catholic nuptial Mass is included on pp. 34-36. But every couple of whatever religious persuasion should consider the possibility of a joyful service of the Lord's Supper, perhaps including fruit and nuts and cheese, or alternatively an agape meal, as part of their wedding. It could simply follow the Affirmation and Pronouncement (p. 24; see outline on p. 7), or it could precede the Affirmation and Pronouncement, coming right after the Blessing and Giving of Rings (p. 23) as an extension of the Ceremony of the Sweet and Bitter Wines (p. 24); it could even be the very first thing in the service. The minister or the song leader could read the story in John 2:1-11 (p. 41) of Jesus turning water into wine at the marriage feast. And someone could read this scripture passage:

> "I come to my garden, my sister, my bride, I gather my myrrh with my spice, I eat my honeycomb with my honey, I drink my wine with my milk. Eat, O friends, and drink: drink deeply, O lovers!" (Song of Solomon 5:1 RSV)

Holy Communion could occur at any point that seems to the bride and groom to best express their joining into a new family, and the whole congregation's joining into a communal fellowship, and Christ's joining us in yet another dimension through our participation in this sacrifice.

THE JOYFUL WEDDING

The essential minimum of a Eucharist (or service of the Lord's Supper or Holy Communion) would simply include the Offertory, the Prayer of Consecration, and the sharing of the elements. But you don't even have to have that in order to share the communal experience of eating something together during the service—bread, cheese, apples, wine—as at an agape meal or "love feast." Agape (pronounced "ah-gah-pay") is a Greek word that means "selfless love" or "holy love," like the love that God has for people. To hold an agape feast, just sing something like "Let Us Break Bread Together," and then do it!

The bride and groom could make all feel welcome to participate by presenting it as their first meal as husband and wife, which they'd like to share with the community. They could invite the guests to particpate in whatever way each felt comfortable, seeing the meal with whatever individual meaning each might bring—a simple sign of community, a sign of the universal food of all mankind, a sign of the Passover meal, a sign of the meal Jesus left as a remembrance.

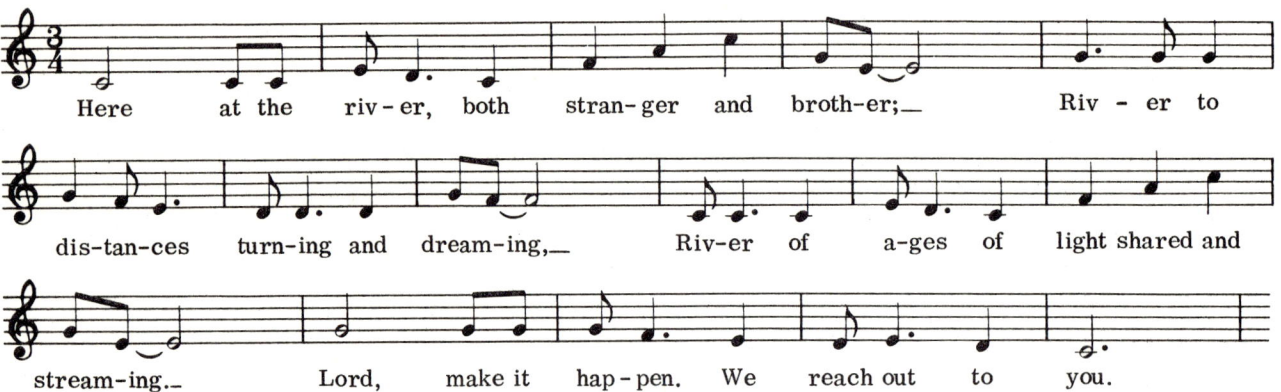

Here at the riv-er, both stran-ger and broth-er;— Riv-er to dis-tan-ces turn-ing and dream-ing,— Riv-er of a-ges of light shared and stream-ing.— Lord, make it hap-pen. We reach out to you.

Outline of the Complete Nuptial Mass

In the historical-sacramental traditions, a complete nuptial Mass or nuptial Eucharist would follow an outline something like this one. Things that are sometimes sung are marked with ♪. Unless indicated to be specific to the Roman Catholic or to the Episcopal tradition, each entry is used by both traditions in their nuptial Mass; the two forms are almost identical.

The ideas presented earlier on how to develop specific elements of the wedding service can be incorporated easily into this framework of the Mass. An original musical setting of the Canon of the Mass can be found on pages 64-71.

♪ Entrance Hymn or Processional (See p. 16.)

  I. *The Entrance Rite or Preparation* (This may be omitted, and the service may begin with II, the Service of the Word of God.)

   A. (Episcopal) The Collect for Purity ("Almighty God, unto whom all hearts are open . . .")
      (Roman Catholic) The Greeting
   B. (Episcopal) The Summary of the Law ("Thou shalt love the Lord thy God . . .")
      (Roman Catholic) The Penitential Rite
      1. Call to Confession
      2. General Confession
      3. Absolution or Assurance of Pardon

THE SERVICE OF HOLY COMMUNION

♪ C. Kyrie Eleison ("Lord, have mercy . . .")
♪ D. Gloria in Excelsis ("Glory to God on High . . .")

II. *The Service of the Word of God* (See p. 17.)
  A. (Episcopal) The Marriage Collect
     (Roman Catholic) Opening Prayers
  B. The Old Testament Lesson
  ♪ C. The Responsorial Psalm
  D. The Epistle
  ♪ E. The Gradual Hymn or the Alleluia
  F. The Gospel
  G. The Sermon or Homily (See p. 18.)

III. *The Rite of Marriage or Solemnization of Matrimony*
  A. The Introduction or Greeting and Preparation (See p. 17.)
  B. The Questioning before the Consent or Charge to the Couple (See p. 17.)
  C. The Consent or Promises and Vows (See pp. 20-23.)
  D. The Blessing and Exchange of Rings (See p. 23.)
  E. (Episcopal) Pronouncement and Nuptial Blessings (See pp. 23-25.)

In some contemporary forms of the Episcopal service, the Celebration and Blessing of a Marriage take the place of the Service of the Word and the Solemnization of Matrimony.

IV. *The Creed and Prayers*
  ♪ A. The Creed or Profession of Faith ("I/We believe in one God . . .")
  B. Prayers of Intercession or Prayer of the Faithful or Prayer for the Church

V. (Episcopal) *The Confession of Sin* (See p. 28.)
  A. Call to Confession
  B. General Confession
  C. Words of Comfort
  D. Absolution or Assurance of Pardon
  ♪ E. The Greeting of Peace (This may be exchanged after the Lord's Prayer, if preferred.) (See p. 26).

In the Episcopal nuptial Mass, the creed, intercessory prayers, and confession may be omitted in contemporary rites, for the wedding is considered to be a festal service.

VI. *The Service of the Lord's Supper* or *Liturgy of the Eucharist* or *Celebration of Holy Communion* (See pp. 29-34.)
  A. The Offertory and Presentation of the gifts of the people and of the bread and wine (See pp. 31-32.)
    ♪ 1. The Offertory hymn
    2. (Roman Catholic) Prayers over the gifts
  B. The Canon of the Mass or the Great Thanksgiving or the Consecration or the Eucharistic Sacrifice
    ♪ 1. The Sursum Corda ("Lift up your hearts . . .")
    ♪ 2. The proper Preface for marriage, ending with "Therefore with Angels and Archangels . . ." (See p. 68.)
    ♪ 3. The Sanctus ("Holy, holy, holy . . .") and Benedictus ("Blessed is he that comes . . .") (See p. 68.)

THE JOYFUL WEDDING

    4. The Prayer of Consecration or the Eucharistic Prayer (various versions)
        a. (Roman Catholic) Special Hanc Igitur for Marriage ("Father, accept this offering . . .")
        ♪ b. The Memorial Acclamation ("Christ has died . . . ," or "When we eat this bread . . . ," etc.) (See p. 70.)
        ♪ c. Concluding Doxology ("Through him, with him, in him . . .") and the Great Amen (See p. 71.)
  C. The Communion Rite (See p. 33.)
    ♪ 1. The Lord's Prayer or Our Father (See p. 26.)
    2. (Roman Catholic) the Nuptial Blessing (See p. 25.)
    ♪ 3. The Greeting of Peace ("Peace be with you . . ."), if not included after the Confession of Sin (V. E.) (See pp. 26-27.)
    4. The Breaking of the Bread
        ♪ a. The Agnus Dei ("Oh Lamb of God . . .") or the "Christ, Our Passover . . ."
        b. The Prayer of Humble Access ("We do not presume to come . . ." or "Lord, I am not worthy . . .")
        c. The Invitation ("The body of our Lord Jesus Christ . . .")
    ♪ 5. The Communion (distribution and partaking of the bread and wine)
    6. Prayer after Communion ("We most heartily thank thee . . ." or "What we have taken like bodily food . . .")

VII. *The Concluding Rite*
  A. The Blessing of the bride and bridegroom, and of the congregation.
  B. The Dismissal ("Go in peace . . ." or "Go forth into the world . . . ," etc.)

♪ Recessional (See p. 27.)

II. SCRIPTURAL REFERENCES WHICH COULD BE USED AT WEDDINGS

Some of these could be read as Scripture lessons, and some could serve as the basis for a meditation or a formal homily or an informal sharing of reflections on marriage during the service; some could be incorporated into the dialogue of the liturgy; some could be printed on the bulletins, invitations, announcements, etc.

I can envisage a wedding ceremony that uses the poetry of the Scriptures in a highly dramatic way, beginning with a——

CALL TO WORSHIP. *Jeremiah 33:10b-11:* "There shall be heard again the voice of mirth and the voice of gladness, the voice of the bridegroom and the voice of the bride, the voices of those who sing." (RSV) (An invitation to pre-service singing.)

BRIDAL PROCESSION. *Psalm 68:24-26:* "Thy solemn processions are seen, O God, the processions of my God, my King, into the sanctuary—the singers in front, the minstrels last, between them maidens playing timbrels: 'Bless God in the great congregation, the Lord, O you who are of Israel's fountain!'" (RSV) *Psalm 57:7b-9:* "I will sing and make melody! Awake my soul! Awake, O harp and lyre! I will awake the dawn! I will give thanks to thee, O Lord, among the peoples; I will sing praises to thee among the nations." (RSV)

ENTRANCE OF THE BRIDE AND GROOM. *Song of Solomon 8:13-14:* "O you who dwell in the gardens, my companions are listening for your voice; let me hear it." The bride's response: "Make haste, my beloved, and be like a gazelle or a young stag upon the mountains of spices." (RSV)

REFLECTIONS ON CREATION. *God creates mankind—Genesis 1:26-31a:* "Then God said, 'Let us make man in our image, after our likeness; and let them have dominion over the fish of the sea, and over the birds of the air, and over the cattle, and over all the earth, and over every creeping thing that creeps upon the earth.' So God created man in his own image, in the image of God he created him; male and female he created them. And God blessed them, and God said to them, 'Be fruitful and multiply, and fill the earth and subdue it; and have dominion over the fish of the sea and over the birds of the air and over every living thing that moves upon the earth.' And God said, 'Behold, I have given you every plant yielding seed which is upon the face of all the earth, and every tree with seed in its fruit; you shall have them for food. And to every beast of the earth, and to every bird of the air, and to everything that creeps on the earth, everything that has the breath of life, I have given every green plant for food.' And it was so. And God saw everything that he had made, and behold, it was very good." (RSV)

THE JOYFUL WEDDING

God creates man more personally, according to a different tradition—Genesis 2:4b-7: "In the day that the Lord God made the earth and the heavens, when no plant of the field was yet in the earth and no herb of the field had yet sprung up—for the Lord God had not caused it to rain upon the earth, and there was no man to till the ground; but a mist went up from the earth and watered the whole face of the ground—then the Lord God formed man of dust from the ground, and breathed into his nostrils the breath of life; and man became a living being." (RSV)

God creates woman—Genesis 2:18-24: "Then the Lord God said, 'It is not good that the man should be alone; I will make him a helper fit for him.' So out of the ground the Lord God formed every beast of the field and every bird of the air, and brought them to the man to see what he would call them; and whatever the man called every living creature, that was its name. The man gave names to all cattle, and to the birds of the air, and to every beast of the field; but for the man there was not found a helper fit for him. So the Lord God caused a deep sleep to fall upon the man, and while he slept took one of his ribs and closed up its place with flesh; and the rib which the Lord God had taken from the man he made into a woman and brought her to the man. Then the man said, 'This at last is bone of my bones and flesh of my flesh; and she shall be called Woman, because she was taken out of Man.' Therefore a man leaves his father and his mother and cleaves to his wife, and they become one flesh." (RSV)

Jesus refers to this passage in Matthew 19:4-6 and in Mark 10:6-8: "Have you not read that he who made them from the beginning made them male and female, and said, 'For this reason a man shall leave his father and mother and be joined to his wife, and the two shall become one flesh'? So they are no longer two but one flesh. What therefore God has joined together, let not man put asunder!" (RSV)

PRAISE OF THE GROOM. *Song of Solomon 2:3-4, 17:* "As an apple tree among the trees of the wood, so is my beloved among young men. With great delight I sat in his shadow, and his fruit was sweet to my taste. He brought me to the banqueting house, and his banner over me was love. . . . Until the day breathes and the shadows flee, turn, my beloved, be like a gazelle, or a young stag upon rugged mountains." (RSV)

Song of Solomon 5:10-16: "My beloved is all radiant and ruddy, distinguished among ten thousand. His head is the finest gold; his locks are wavy, black as a raven. His eyes are like doves beside springs of water, bathed in milk, fitly set. His cheeks are like beds of spices, yielding fragrance. His lips are lilies, distilling liquid myrrh. His arms are rounded gold, set with jewels. His body is ivory work, encrusted with sapphires. His legs are alabaster columns, set upon bases of gold. His appearance is like Lebanon, choice as the cedars. His speech is most sweet, and he is altogether desirable. This is my beloved and this my friend, O daughters of Jerusalem." (RSV)

PRAISE OF THE BRIDE. *Song of Solomon 7:1-5:* "How graceful are your feet in sandals, O queenly maiden! Your rounded thighs are like jewels, the work of a master hand. Your navel is a rounded bowl that never lacks mixed wine. Your belly is a heap of wheat, encircled with lilies. Your two breasts are like two fawns, twins of a gazelle. Your neck is like an ivory tower. Your eyes are pools in Heshbon, by the gate of Bathrabbim. Your nose is like a tower of Lebanon, overlooking Damascus. Your head crowns you like Carmel, and your flowing locks are like purple; a king is held captive in the tresses." (RSV)

Song of Solomon 7:6-9: "How fair and pleasant you are, O loved one, delectable maiden! You

SCRIPTURAL REFERENCES

are stately as a palm tree, and your breasts are like its clusters. I say I will climb the palm tree and lay hold of its branches. Oh, may your breasts be like clusters of the vine, and the scent of your breath like apples, and your kisses like the best wine that goes down smoothly, gliding over lips and teeth." (RSV)

A beautiful encomium to the ideal wife—Proverbs 31:10-13, 17, 20, 25-29: "A good wife who can find? She is far more precious than jewels. The heart of her husband trusts in her, and he will have no lack of gain. She does him good, and not harm, all the days of her life. She seeks wood and flax, and works with willing hands. . . . She girds her loins with strength and makes her arms strong. . . . She opens her hand to the poor, and reaches out her hands to the needy. . . . Strength and dignity are her clothing, and she laughs at the time to come. She opens her mouth with wisdom, and the teaching of kindness is on her tongue. She looks well to the ways of her household, and does not eat the bread of idleness. Her children rise up and call her blessed; her husband also, and he praises her: 'Many women have done excellently, but you surpass them all.' " (RSV)

PRAISE OF THE CONGREGATION. *Isaiah 62:5.* "As the bridegroom rejoices over the bride, so shall your God rejoice over you." (RSV)

PRAISE OF THE INSTITUTION OF MARRIAGE. *Hebrews 13:4:* "Let marriage be held in honor among all, and let husbands and wives be faithful to each other, for God will judge the immoral and adulterous." (Also see *Genesis 2:18-24, Matthew 19:4-6, Mark 10:6-8.*)

Ecclesiastes 4:7-12. (This is my very favorite Bible passage on the beauty—and necessity—of human fellowship. These words are set to music in the song called "The Raddle of Love," p. 52.): "Again, I saw vanity under the sun: a person who has no one, either son or brother, yet there is no end to all his toil, and his eyes are never satisfied with riches, so that he never asks, 'For whom am I toiling and depriving myself of pleasure?' This also is vanity and an unhappy business.

"Two are better than one, because they have a good reward for their toil. For if they fall, one will lift up his fellow; but woe to him who is alone when he falls and has not another to lift him up. Again, if two lie together, they are warm; but how can one be warm alone? And though a man might prevail against one who is alone, two will withstand him. A threefold cord is not quickly broken." (RSV)

PREPARATION FOR LEAVE-TAKING. *Song of Solomon 6:9:* "My dove, my perfect one, is only one, the darling of her mother, flawless to her that bore her." (RSV)

Also *Matthew 19:4-5:* "He answered, 'Have you not read that he who made them from the beginning made them male and female, and said, For this reason a man shall leave his father and mother and be joined to his wife, and the two shall become one flesh'?" (RSV)

Also *Genesis 2:24:* "Therefore a man leaves his father and his mother and cleaves to his wife, and they become one flesh." (RSV)

TENDER EXPRESSION OF LOVE. (*Of all the fragments in the Song of Solomon, I find this the loveliest.*) *Song of Solomon 2:10-13:* "Rise up, my love, my fair one, and come away. For lo, the winter is past, the rain is over and gone. The flowers appear on the earth, the time of singing of birds is come, and the voice of the turtle is heard in our land. The fig tree putteth forth her green figs, and the vines with the tender grape give a good smell. Arise, my love, my fair one, and come away." (KJV)

THE JOYFUL WEDDING

MEDITATIONS ON LOVE AND MARRIAGE

a) I Corinthians 13:1-13—Paul's famous essay on love, the greatest of the gifts of the Spirit: "If I speak in the tongues of men and of angels, but have not love, I am a noisy gong or a clanging cymbal. And if I have prophetic powers, and understand all mysteries and all knowledge, and if I have all faith, so as to remove mountains, but have not love, I am nothing. I may give away everything I have, and even give up my body to be burned—but if I have not love, it does me no good.

"Love is patient and kind; love is not jealous or boastful; it is not arrogant or rude. Love does not insist on its own way; it is not irritable or resentful; it does not rejoice at wrong, but rejoices in the right. Love bears all things, believes all things, hopes all things, endures all things.

"Love never ends. There are inspired messages, but they are temporary; there are gifts of speaking in strange tongues, but they will cease; there is knowledge, but it will pass away. For our gifts of knowledge and of inspired messages are only partial; but when what is perfect comes, then what is partial will disappear.

"When I was a child, I spoke like a child, I thought like a child, I reasoned like a child; when I became a man, I gave up childish ways. What we see now is like the dim image in a mirror; then we shall see face to face. What I know now is only partial; then it will be complete, as complete as God's knowledge of me.

"Meanwhile these three remain: faith, hope, and love; and the greatest of these is love."

b) I Corinthians 7:3-4—the equality of conjugal rights, and the need for mutual consideration in the physical relationship: "The husband should give to his wife her conjugal rights, and likewise the wife to her husband and each should satisfy the other's needs. The wife has no longer full rights over her own person, but shares them with her husband. In the same way the husband shares his personal rights with his wife."

c) Ephesians 5:22-25, 28-29—the marriage relationship in the Christian household; the keynote is mutual subjugation, and responsibility for cherishing and protecting: "You wives must learn to adapt yourselves to your husbands, as you submit yourselves to the Lord, for the husband is the 'head' of the wife in the same way that Christ is head of the Church and savior of the body. The willing subjection of the Church to Christ should be reproduced in the submission of wives to their husbands. But, remember, this means that the husband must give his wife the same sort of love that Christ gave to the Church, when he sacrificed himself for her. . . .

"Men ought to give their wives the love they naturally have for their own bodies. The love a man gives his wife is the extending of his love for himself to enfold her. Nobody ever hates or neglects his own body; he feeds it and looks after it. And that is what Christ does for his body, the Church." (Phillips)

d) Matthew 5:31-32—permanence of marriage, and views on divorce and re-marriage: "It was also said, 'Anyone who divorces his wife must give her a written notice of divorce.' But now I tell you: If a man divorces his wife, and she has not been unfaithful, then he is guilty of making her commit adultery if she marries again; and the man who marries her also commits adultery." (TEV)

Mark 10:2-12: "Then some Pharisees arrived to ask him this test question, 'Is it right for a man to divorce his wife?' Jesus replied by asking them, 'What has Moses commanded you to do?' 'Moses allows man to write a divorce notice and then to dismiss her,' they said. 'Moses gave you that commandment,' returned Jesus, 'because you know so little of the meaning of love. But from the beginning of the creation, God made them male and female. "For this cause shall a man leave

SCRIPTURAL REFERENCES

his father and mother, and shall cleave to his wife; and the twain shall become one flesh." So that in body they are no longer two people but one. That is why man must never separate what God has joined together.'

"On reaching the house, his disciples questioned him again about this matter. 'Any man who divorces his wife and marries another woman,' he told them, 'commits adultery against his wife. And if she herself divorces her husband and marries someone else, she commits adultery.' " (Phillips)

Romans 7:1-3: "You know very well, my brothers (for I am speaking to those well acquainted with the subject), that the Law can only exercise authority over a man so long as he is alive. A married woman, for example, is bound by the Law to her husband so long as he is alive. But if he dies, then his legal claim over her disappears. This means that, if she should give herself to another man while her husband is alive, she incurs the stigma of adultery. But if, after her husband's death, she does exactly the same thing, no one could call her an adulteress, for the Law's hold over her has been dissolved by her husband's death." (Phillips)

I Corinthians 7:10: "To those who are already married my command, or rather, the Lord's command, is that the wife should not leave her husband. But if she is separated from him she should either remain unattached or else be reconciled to her husband. A husband is not, in similar circumstances, to divorce his wife." (Phillips)

e) *John 2:1-11—Jesus at the wedding feast at Cana, performing "the first of his signs":* "Two days later there was a wedding in the Galilean village of Cana. Jesus' mother was there and he and his disciples were invited to the festivities. Then it happened that the supply of wine gave out, and Jesus' mother told him, 'They have no more wine.' 'Is that your concern, or mine?' replied Jesus. 'My time has not come yet.' So his mother said to the servants, 'Mind you do whatever he tells you.'

"In the room six very large stone water jars stood on the floor (actually for the Jewish ceremonial cleansing), each holding about twenty gallons. Jesus gave instructions for these jars to be filled with water, and the servants filled them to the brim. Then he said to them, 'Now draw some out and take it to the master of ceremonies,' which they did. When this man tasted the water, which had now become wine, without knowing where it came from (though naturally the servants who had drawn the water knew), he called out to the bridegroom and said to him, 'Everybody I know puts his good wine on first and then when men have had plenty to drink, he brings out the poor stuff. But you have kept back your good wine till now!' Jesus gave this, the first of his signs, at Cana in Galilee." (Phillips)

FOR AN AGAPE FEAST (or for the reception). *Song of Solomon 5:1:* "I come to my garden, my sister, my bride, I gather my myrrh with my spice, I eat my honeycomb with my honey, I drink my wine with my milk. Eat, O friends, and drink: drink deeply, O lovers!" (RSV)

FOR HOLY COMMUNION

a) *Accounts of the Last Supper* appear in *Matthew 26:26-30, Mark 14:22-26,* and *Luke 22:14-23. John 13:1-30* follows a different tradition.

b) *Paul's interpretations of the Lord's Supper* are set forth in *I Corinthians 10:16-17:* "When we bless 'the cup of blessing,' is it not a participation in the blood of Christ? When we break the bread, is it not a participation in the body of Christ? The very fact that we all share one loaf makes us all one body."

THE JOYFUL WEDDING

And in I Corinthians 11:23-26: "The teaching I gave you was given me personally by the Lord himself, and it was this: the Lord Jesus, in the same night in which he was betrayed, took bread, and when he had given thanks he broke it, and said, 'Take, eat, this is my body, which is being broken for you. Do this in remembrance of me.' Similarly when supper was ended, he took the cup saying, 'This cup is the new agreement in my blood: do this, whenever you drink it, in remembrance of me.' . . . Whenever you eat this bread or drink of this cup, you are proclaiming that the Lord has died for you, and you will do that until he comes again." (Phillips)

c) *John's interpretation of Jesus as the Messianic manna is found in John 6:35-36:* "I am the bread of life; he who comes to me shall never hunger" and in *6:48-58:* "I am the living bread which came down from heaven; . . . he who eats my flesh and drinks my blood has eternal life."

d) *Jesus reveals himself through breaking bread with people in Luke 24:13-35, in the encounter on the road to Emmaus:* "And when he had sat down with them at table, he took bread and said the blessing; he broke the bread, and offered it to them. Then their eyes were opened, and they recognized him. . . . Then they gave their account of the events of their journey, and told how he had been recognized by them at the breaking of the bread." (NEB) *And in Revelation 3:20:* "Behold, I stand at the door and knock; if anyone hears my voice and opens the door, I will come in to him and eat with him, and he with me." (RSV)

e) *One of the many references to the simple goodness of food and drink is found in Psalm 104:13-15:* "Thou dost cause the grass to grow for the cattle, and plants for man to cultivate, that he may bring forth food from the earth, and wine to gladden the heart of man, oil to make his face shine, and bread to strengthen a man's heart." (RSV)

VOWS AND STATEMENTS OF COMMITMENT. *Hosea 2:19:* "I will betroth you to me forever; I will betroth you to me in righteousness and in justice, in steadfast love, and in mercy." (RSV)

Ruth 1:16-17: "Entreat me not to leave thee, or to return from following after thee; for whither thou goest, I will go; and where thou lodgest, I will lodge: thy people shall be my people, and thy God my God: Where thou diest, will I die, and there will I be buried: the Lord do so to me, and more also, if aught but death part thee and me." (KJV)

AFFIRMATION. *Ecclesiastes 9:9:* "Enjoy life with the wife whom you love, all the days of your . . . life which he has given you under the sun, because that is your portion in life." (RSV)

RECESSIONAL. *Song of Solomon 7:11-12:* "Come, my beloved, let us go forth into the fields, and lodge in the villages; let us go out early to the vineyards, and see whether the vines have budded, whether the grape blossoms have opened and the pomegranates are in bloom. There I will give you my love." (RSV)

A Note on the Song of Solomon

The Song of Solomon, that most curious of the books of the Old Testament canon, is a collection of about twenty-five songs and song fragments meant to be sung at weddings—a sort of third-century B.C. "Joyful Wedding." This pure erotic celebration of the physical beauty with which two lovers see each other may be a little heady for most contemporary styles—but maybe it's time to break out of contemporary style and get a little more into the graceful, sensual eros that we see revealed in these poems.

SCRIPTURAL REFERENCES

Having Found Some Unused Space . . .

Here is a list of some other songs from the secular sphere which we have used in weddings:

"Black Is the Color of My True Love's Hair" (Appalachian folk song)
"What Wondrous Love Is This?" (Southern folk hymn)
"Sunrise, Sunset" (from *Fiddler on the Roof*, by Sheldon Harnick and Jerry Bock)
"One Hand, One Heart" (from *West Side Story*, by Steven Sondheim and Leonard Bernstein)
"If We Only Have Love" (by Jacques Brel)
"Today" (by Randy Sparks)
"The Wedding Song" (popularized by Paul Stookey)
"Follow Me" (by John Denver; popularized by Mary Travers)
"The Song Is Love" (by Stookey, Yarrow, Travers, Dixon, and Kniss; popularized by Peter, Paul and Mary)
"We've Only Just Begun to Live" (by Roger Nicholas and Paul Williams; popularized by The Carpenters)

III. NEW MUSIC FOR WEDDINGS

Joy Is Now

Words and Music by Phil West
and Ann Grant

Joy is now, joy is here, joy is danc-ing to a

Harmony lines for any combination of instruments or voices singing "Ah."

beat the wind can hear. Joy is breath-ing in the sun-shine, joy is

laugh-ing in the rain. Joy is be-ing some-one pray-ing stand-ing near.

Fine

* Use alternate verses and setting by Nick Hodsdon
at this point, if desired. See page 45.

1. When I was ver-y young, I learned to say a prayer at the

end of ev-ery day, but child-ish words are lost in mem-o-

ry, and now a new prayer makes more sense to me.

D.C.

© 1969 by Ann Grant and Phil West. Harmony © 1973 by Nick Hodsdon.

44

2. I've come a long way since I was a child.
   I gave up church when people called me wild.
   My mind's been changed by many things I've seen,
   I found the feelings echo in my dreams.

3. I've walked the streets of London and Belgrade.
   I've slept on beaches, in fields and empty barns;
   I've read the New York Times in Tel Aviv,
   and wand'ring made me ready to believe.

4. I'd never call it off and go back home.
   Protect, intend, pretending on the phone.
   I'll never be the child I was before,
   I think God made my life for something more.

© 1969 Ann Grant & Phil West

Joy Is Now

A good processional hymn. Phil West and his wife, Ann Grant, wrote the tune and most of the chorus for this one. I added verses when Pat Hall asked me to write a joyful opening hymn for her wedding. The verses are about as close as I've ever come to writing a statement of my personal theology. These verses come right after the words, "Joy is being someone praying, standing near" in the chorus.

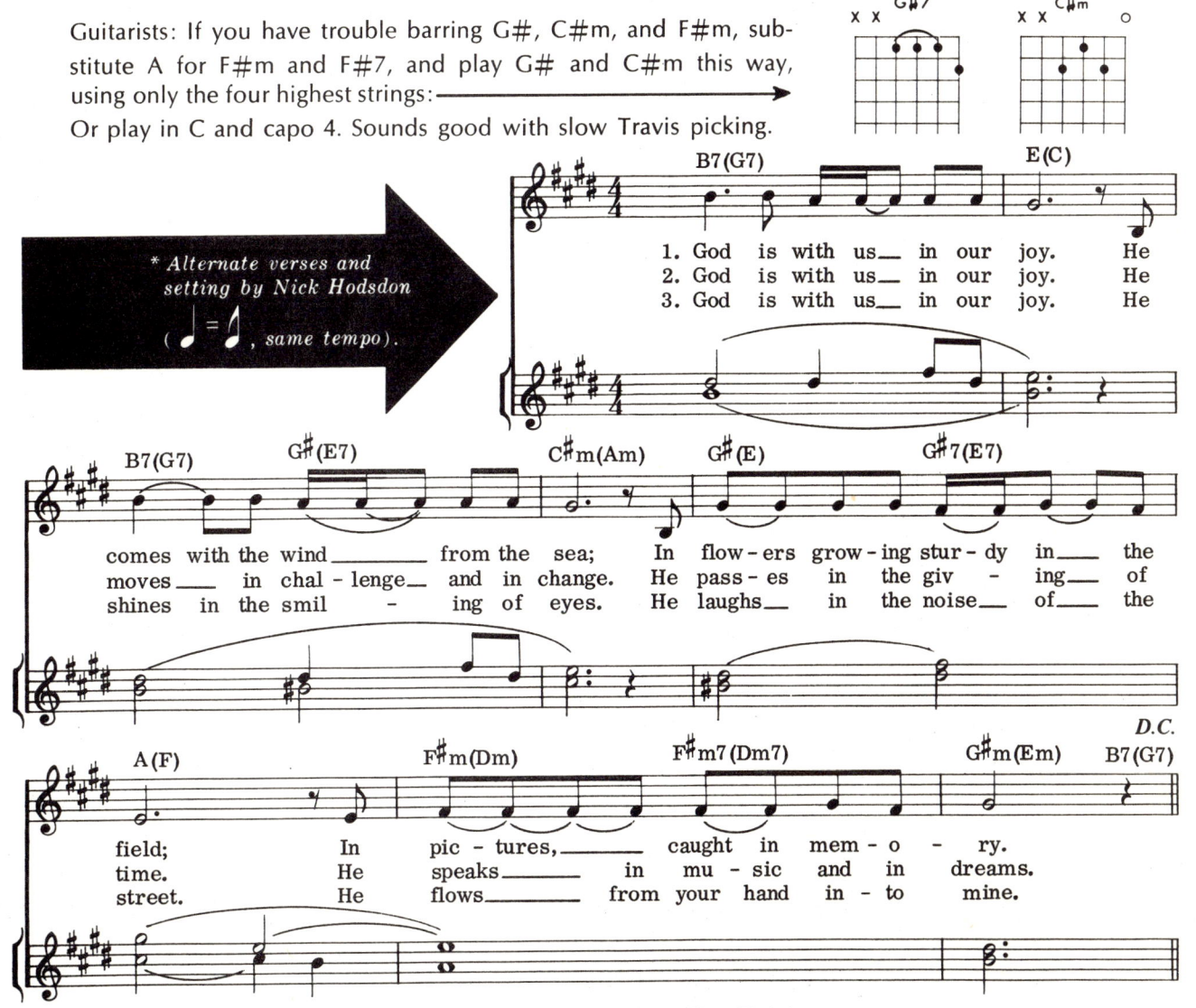

Guitarists: If you have trouble barring G#, C#m, and F#m, substitute A for F#m and F#7, and play G# and C#m this way, using only the four highest strings:⟶
Or play in C and capo 4. Sounds good with slow Travis picking.

*Alternate verses and setting by Nick Hodsdon
(♩ = ♩, same tempo).

1. God is with us in our joy. He comes with the wind from the sea; In flow-ers grow-ing stur-dy in the field; In pic-tures, caught in mem-o-ry.
2. God is with us in our joy. He moves in chal-lenge and in change. He pass-es in the giv-ing of time. He speaks in mu-sic and in dreams.
3. God is with us in our joy. He shines in the smil-ing of eyes. He laughs in the noise of the street. He flows from your hand in-to mine.

Words and arrangement © 1970 by Nick Hodsdon.

Man Is the Joy of Man

    This song was written as a wedding gift for Phil West and Ann Grant, when Phil and I were students at Union Seminary in New York City and I couldn't afford to buy him anything worthwhile.

    The text comes from Norse wisdom literature, similar to the Hebrew Book of Proverbs, which was included in an ancient collection of Nordic myths, "wise sayings," songs, and stories written down in Iceland and called the *Elder Edda*. And now, let me turn you all on to some really good things in Norse mythology (of all things). When I was a little kid I first discovered the world of Odin and Fricka and Fasalt and Faffner; in my first year of seminary I discovered the *Elder Edda*, and "Man Is the Joy of Man" happened.

    These anonymous poets of Norse mythology are the only extant spokesmen for the ancient beliefs of the whole great Teutonic race, of which England and, through our first settlers, America too is a part. Everywhere else in northwestern Europe the early native records, songs, and stories were obliterated by the Latin-speaking priests of Christianity, who felt a bitter hatred for the paganism they had come to destroy. Only a few bits escaped destruction—*Beowulf* in England, the *Nibelungenlied* in Germany. But by the eleventh century, when the Christian missionaries finally reached Iceland, their destructive zeal seems to have abated. Latin didn't replace Norse as the literary tongue, and the materials which were later collected into the *Elder* and *Younger Eddas* survived. The earliest manuscript of the *Elder Edda* is dated about 1300, but its poems are much older, from centuries of circulation in Icelandic oral tradition. It's kind of nice that this collection of songs to be used in Catholic, Protestant, Jewish, and maybe even nonreligious wedding ceremonies should begin with reworked poems from an ancient "pagan" tradition.

    The feelings and thoughts of love between husband and wife, between friend and friend, are ancient, modern, cross-cultural, and universal. In the Song of Solomon, which also draws on ancient "pagan" mythology, the bride says of her bridegroom, "This is my beloved and this is my friend, O daughters of Jerusalem!" And Maxim Gorky caught it when in 1907 he wrote, "There will come a time, I know, when people will take delight in one another, when each will be a star to the other, and when each will listen to his fellow as to music."

    People seem to like this song around campfires or at communal sing-ins as much as at weddings. We usually repeat the chorus after the first verse, and again at the end. After the first verse or so, you may wish to add some touches of harmony, such as—

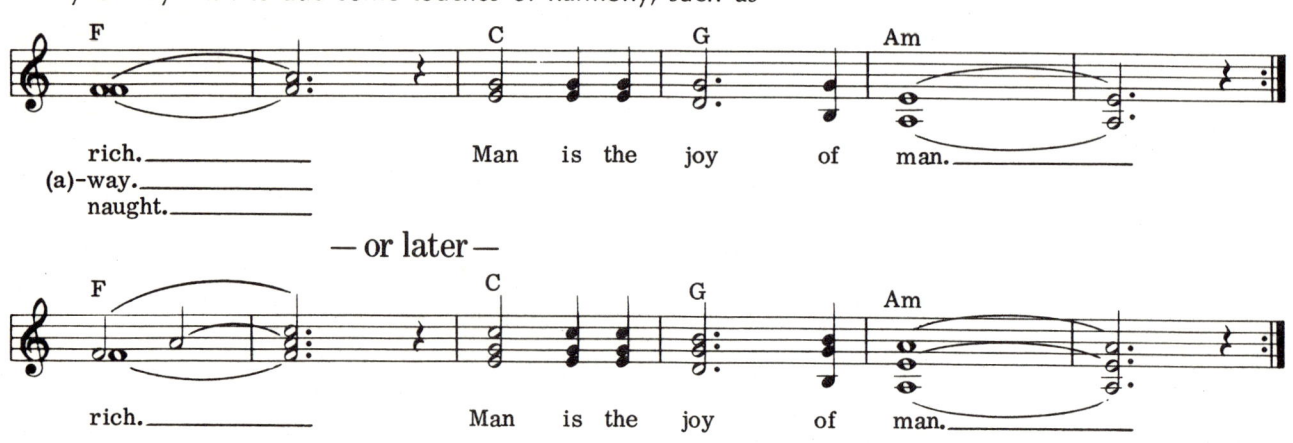

[musical notation: F C G Am — "rich. / (a)-way. / naught. ... Man is the joy of man."]

— or later —

[musical notation: F C G Am — "rich. ... Man is the joy of man."]

Guitarists: This is easiest to play in C, but it will be easier to sing if you capo it up two frets or so. It sounds good with a lot of hammer-stroking.

Man Is the Joy of Man

A Hymn for Weddings and Other Communal Occasions

(A wedding gift for Phil West and Ann Grant)

Text adapted from *The Elder Edda*
Guitar: capo 2 (sing in D)

Words and music by Nick Hodsdon

Quietly

(Introduction)

Chorus: When I was young, I trav-eled a - lone. When
1. To a good friend's house, the road is straight. To a
2. None so good, that he has no fault.
3. Cat - tle die, and kin - dred die.

I was young, I trav-eled a - lone. When
good friend's house, the road is straight. To a
None so good, that he has no fault.
Cat - tle die, and kin - dred die.

I was young I trav - eled a - lone, I met an -
good friend's house the road is straight, Though
None so good that he has no fault, None so
Cat - tle die and kin - dred die, but I know one

oth - er and I found I was rich. Man is the joy of man. 1. To a
he is far a - way. Man is the joy of man. (Cho.) When
wick-ed that he is worth naught. Man is the joy of man. (Cho.) When
thing that nev - er dies: The joy that man gives to man. (Cho.) When

47

Love Is a Double Helix

    Clotho, Lachesis, and Atropos were the Three Fates of classical mythology. Clotho spun the thread of life, Lachesis determined its length, and Atropos cut it off when life was completed. The lives of people who love seem to circle and support each other in a helical pattern, rather like the structure of the DNA molecule (a double helix)—the chemical of life and heredity, bringing fruit which bears seed (Genesis 1:11-12, 28-29). But the love and the lives don't seem to turn inward, but circle out into the vineyard of life and other people and work and friendship. Three days before his wedding, a friend from the vineyard called long distance to remind me that I had promised to write him a song for his marriage. Stuck for something to write, I got him and his fiancée to free-associate about what marriage meant, and this song was the hasty result.

    The quotation in the last verse is from a poem by e. e. cummings. If anybody knows the Hellenistic poet who wrote the poem on which the chorus is based, please write and let me know! I remember the poem from a junior high school Latin class, but I can't find the original source.

    This song works best as a solo or choir thing, with congregation joining in on the chorus. Harmonize ad libitum.

Guitarists: Speaking of harmony, you'll find that playing all the chords in regular open-string positions will create rather horrendous discords with the vocal line. To cancel this out, A6 and Am6 should be played in the unorthodox fashions indicated. And, if you have trouble with Emaj7, just play a plain E. Try it with a Travis pick.

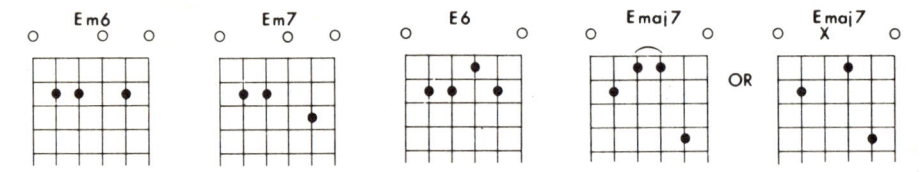

[Chord diagrams: Em6, Em7, E6, Emaj7, OR Emaj7]

If you prefer to play in the key of A and capo it up to a comfortable pitch, use these chords:

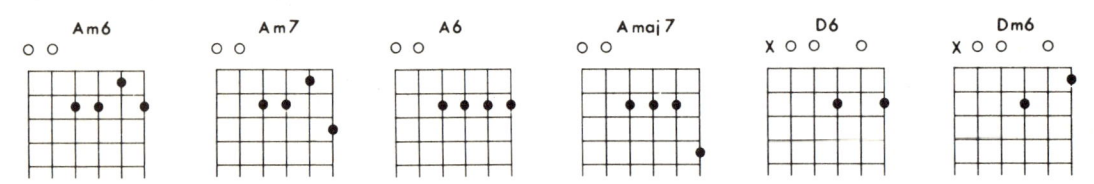

[Chord diagrams: Am6, Am7, A6, Amaj7, D6, Dm6]

Love Is a Double Helix
(A wedding gift for John and Elain Thellman)

To sing in a lower key, use chords in parentheses and capo 2 or 3.

Words and music by Nick Hodsdon

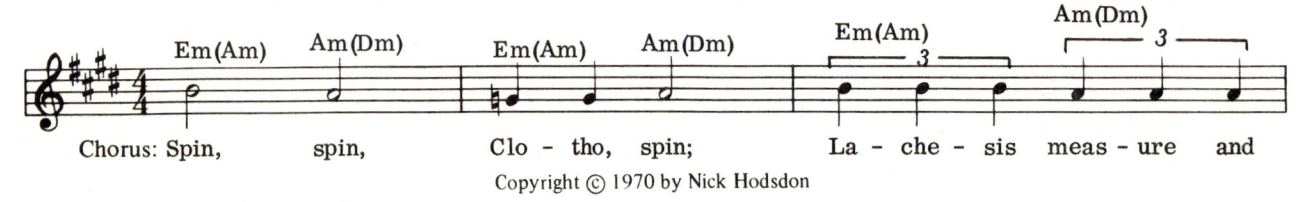

[Musical notation with chords: Em(Am), Am(Dm), Em(Am), Am(Dm), Em(Am), Am(Dm)]

Chorus: Spin, spin, Clo - tho, spin; La - che - sis meas - ure and

Copyright © 1970 by Nick Hodsdon

Em(Am) B7(E7) Em(Am) Em6(Am6) Em7(Am7) Em6(Am6)
At - ro - pos sev - er the vine.
E(A) A(D) E(A) A(D) E(A) A(D)
Spin, spin, Clo - tho, spin; La - che - sis meas - ure and
last time to CODA
E(A) B7(E7) 1, 2, 3. E(A) E6(A6) Emaj7(Amaj7)
At - ro - pos sev - er the vine.
E6 (A6) A(D) A6 (D6) Am6 (Dm6)
1. And the vine cir - cles 'round, weaves its spell, weaves its
2. Peo - ple grow, cir - cle 'round, to em - brace, to sus-
3. Then the vine reach - es out to em - brace, to en-
E6(A6) A(D) B7(E7) E(A)
love And we're bound in the skein of the vine.
tain And are held in the skein of the vine.
fold, Each to give, each re - ceive, in the vine.
E6(A6) Emaj7(Amaj7) E6(A6) A(D) A6(D6)
And the strength from a - bove to the
Bend and turn to up - hold, weave a
"For love is in we are in
Am6(Dm6) E(A) A(D) B7(E7) D.C. E(A) E6(A6)
root through the leaves brings the fruit with its seed for the vine.
cord, in - ter - twine. One times one still is one in the vine.
I am in you" And we're bound in the skein of the vine.
CODA
E(A) E6(A6) Emaj7 (Amaj7) E6(A6) A(D) B7(E7)
vine. And we're bound in the skein of the
E(A) E6(A6) Emaj7(Amaj7) E6(A6) E(A) E6(A6) E(A) E(A)
vine.

Into Living

My friend and sustainer, Sandy Lloyd, asked me to write her a song for her birthday. At the same time, we were preparing a series of folk services for a nice but rather uptight Methodist church in Middletown, New York, whose members thought of a loving response to God only in terms of things like pledging money for an expensive new church organ, and not in terms of giving time and thought and energy to the needs of the people of their community. We thought about just what it was that God wanted from people, and looked up what the prophet Micah had to say about it 2,700 years ago. He asks: What does the Lord require? How do you want me? How should I stand?

"With what shall I come before the Lord, and bow myself before God on high? Shall I come before him with burnt offerings, with calves a year old? Will the Lord be pleased with thousands of rams, with ten thousands of rivers of oil?" (Micah 6:6-7a RSV.)

The prophet answers his own question: "He has showed you, O man, what is good; and what does the Lord require of you but to do justice, and to love kindness, and to walk humbly with your God?" (Micah 6:8 RSV.)

We compared what John wrote about it, 800 years later:

> You must not be surprised, brothers, when the world condemns you; we have passed out of death and into life, and of this we can be sure because we love our brothers. . . . If a man who was rich enough in the world's goods saw that one of his brothers was in need, but closed his heart to him, how could the love of God be living in him? My children, our love is not to be just words or mere talk, but something real and active; only by this can we be certain that we are children of the truth and be able to quieten our conscience in his presence, whenever our hearts condemn us, because God is greater than our conscience, and he knows everything. (I John 3:13-14, 17-20 from JB and RSV; see *Offertory*, pp. 31-32.)

I think that one would do best to come to man—to a loving friend, man or woman; to husband or wife; to bride or groom—with the same things that God wanted. So for Sandy's birthday I put it all together as best I could in "Into Living." It's meant to serve either as a prayer or as a love song.

Guitarists: To make a C9, just make a C and then put your pinkie down on the second string. If you have as much trouble playing C6 as I do, just substitute an Am. (Note: C/B means a C chord with a B in the bass.)

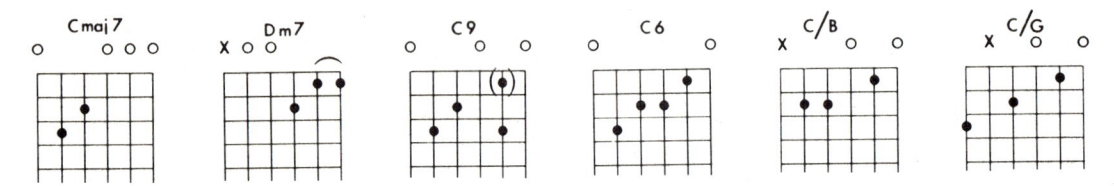

Into Living
For Sandy Lloyd

Micah 6:6 - 8
1 John 3:13 - 20a

Words and music by Nick Hodsdon

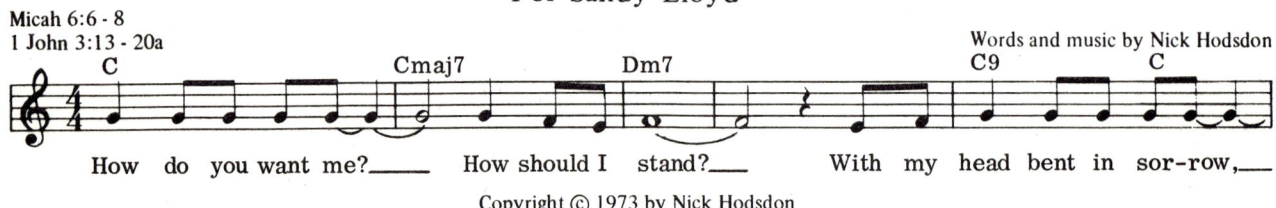

How do you want me?____ How should I stand?___ With my head bent in sor-row,___

Copyright © 1973 by Nick Hodsdon

Cmaj7 C6 Dm7 C C/B Am C/G
with alms in my hand? In my weak-ness, in my strength, with my
F Dm7 G7 C Cmaj7
arms out to love you? How shall I love you, wrong as I
Dm7 C9 C Cmaj7 C6 Dm7
am, with my heart's un-der-stand-ing, to share what I am,
C C/B Am C/G F
all un - fold - ing; need - ing, too; and in giv - ing, re - ceiv - ing.
Dm7 G7 C Cmaj7 Dm7
If my heart should con-demn me, by this I will stand
C9 C Cmaj7 C6 Dm7
out of death, in - to liv - ing, to love as a man, meet your
C C/B Am C/G F Dm7 G7
need - ing; just in deed; walk - ing hum - bly be - side you. If the
C C/B Am Fm C
world should con-demn me, by this I will stand: in my weak - ness,
C/B Am Am7 F Em
in my strength, with my arms out to love you.
Dm7 G7 Cmaj7 Dm7 Fm Fm6 Cmaj7
(instrumental)

The Raddle of Love

The text for this song comes from an anonymous philosopher who wrote in the third century B.C. It's the best passage on human companionship that I've ever found in the Bible, by the same author who wrote, "For everything there is a season, and a time for every purpose under heaven." The biblical text can be found on p. 39.

A good friend of mine, another former fellow seminary student, invited me and about a dozen more of his friends to come share the last three days of his honeymoon with him and his wife in a cabin in Vermont. That first night I couldn't stop thinking about how the people there cared about and supported each other, and how the love that each of us had to give circled around and came back to us so much stronger, and how great it was to be a part of something like this. So that night I wrote this for Carl and Carol, and for all the rest of us, and for my roommate, and for another couple whose wedding was coming up.

This song works well as a hymn which a congregation can learn quickly, supported by a few people singing the harmony (given on p. 54). Or a small group could sing it just before the promises and vows, as a meditation on marriage. It should start quietly, and become really full-bodied by the last verse. If they can manage it, harmony people should go back to singing melody on the fourth verse, and break into harmony on the words "So love must expand."

In a nuptial Mass, the first two verses could be sung after the Epistle (maybe substituting Genesis 2:4b-7, 18-25), and the last two verses after the Gospel (Jesus reiterates the Genesis passage in Matthew 19:4-6).

Guitarists: If you have trouble with F#m, substitute A instead. If you can't barre the G#7 and C#m, play them this way, using only the 4 highest strings.

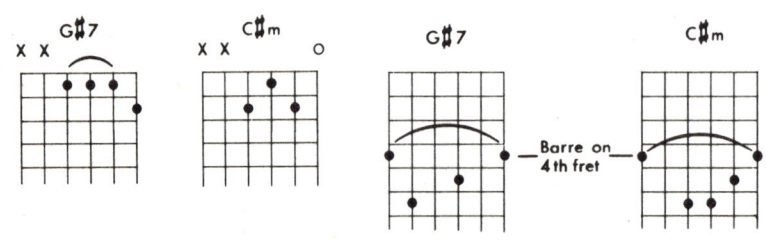

The Raddle* of Love

Ecclesiastes 4:7 - 12

Words and music by Nick Hodsdon

1. A - gain I saw van - i - ty un - der the sun: A man with no broth - er, no part - ner, no son; Yet there is no end to all his toil - ing; His rich - es to ash - es, his hap - pi - ness foil - ing. "For whom am I toil - ing un - der the sun?"

2. Two work - ing to - geth - er are bet - ter than one. They share the re - ward as the life - bond is spun. For if they should fall, one will lift up the oth - er, But sor - row to him with no part - ner or broth - er To lift him, in lone - fall - ing un - der the sun.

3. If two lie to - geth - er, how warm they will be! But cold is the night of the man whol - ly free, With no one to need him, de - pend on him, feed him, With love and com - mun - ion, to fol - low and lead him As love moves the two to a chord that is three.

4. Then joy will reach out in the rad - dle of love To fill and re - sound, re - turn high a - bove. So love must ex - pand to vi - brate in oth - ers; The hard, joy - ous ven - ture of liv - ing to - geth - er Grows rich - er three - fold with the spir - it a - bove;

Grows vi - brant and strong, a rad - dle of love.

(* "Raddle" means to interweave, twine together.)

Copyright © 1970 by Nick Hodsdon

Harmony lines to be added on verses 2, 3, and 4, for any combination of voices or instruments.

2. Two working together are better than one. They share the reward as the life-bond is spun. For if they should fall, one will lift up the other, But sorrow to him with no partner or brother To lift him, in lone-falling under the sun.

3. If two lie together, how warm they will be! But cold is the night of the man wholly free, With no one to need him, depend on him, feed him With love and communion, to follow and lead him, As love moves the two to a chord that is three.

4. Then joy will reach out in the raddle of love To fill and resound, return high above. So love must expand to vibrate in others; The hard, joyous venture of living together Grows richer three-fold with the spirit above;

Grows vibrant and strong, a raddle of love.

54

Unfolding

I originally wrote this as a birthday song for a guitar student who had just turned thirteen, and for my father, who had just turned sixty-two. It can be used as a universal rite of passage song—change a few words in the second verse and it's a wedding song, a New Year's song, a song for a new birth. The tune for this one is based on one of the hundred-odd versions of the ballad of Jimmy Grove and Barbara Allan. It can come right after the exchange of rings, or between the prayers of blessing, or right after the pronouncement. Or it can be used as a quieter, slower-tempoed, more reflective processional.

Congregations usually need to have the music for this one, or to hear the melody a couple of times before they can sing it. It sounds best when lower voices sing the descant *below* the melody. It's especially effective if you play a measure of B7 before singing "A wedding . . ." and then do the second verse in the key of E; play a measure of A7 before singing "Friends fall a-. . ." and do the third verse in the key of D; then play a measure of D7 and repeat the third verse in the key of G again. Congregations can follow this sort of thing pretty well, if they can hear the instruments warning them that a modulation is coming, and if somebody starts them on the right note.

Chord sequence in E:
 B7—E—Emaj7—C#m—Emaj7—E—B7—E—Emaj7—C#m——G#m——A—Amaj7—F#m—B7—E.
Chord sequence in D:
 A7—D—Dmaj7—Bm—Dmaj7—D—A7—D—Dmaj7—Bm——F#m——G—Gmaj7—Em—A7—D.
If you have trouble barring a Bm, play this:

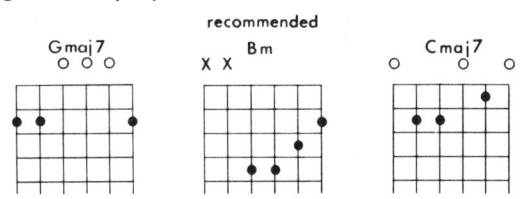

MUSIC ON PAGE 56

Unfolding

Words by Nick Hodsdon

Tune based on a traditional ballad
Arranged by Nick Hodsdon

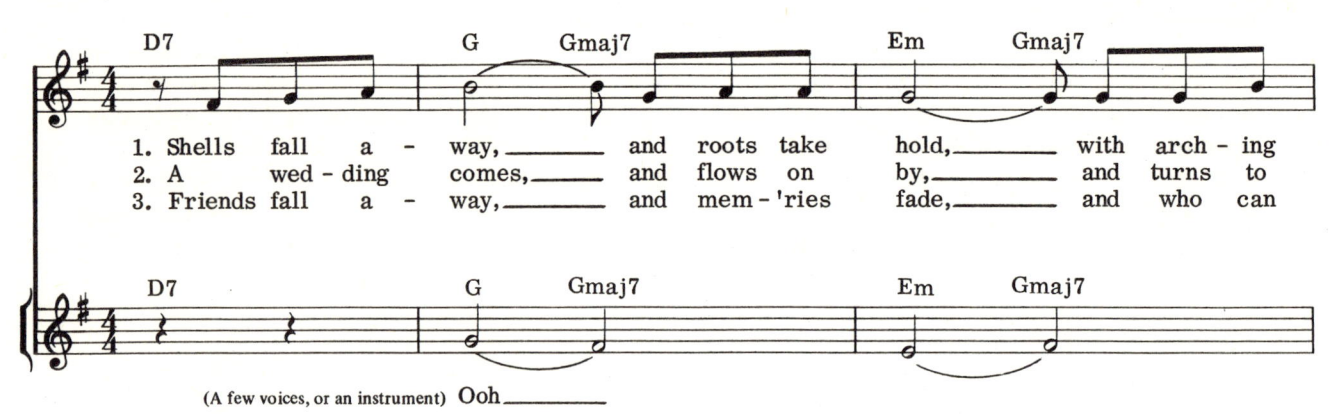

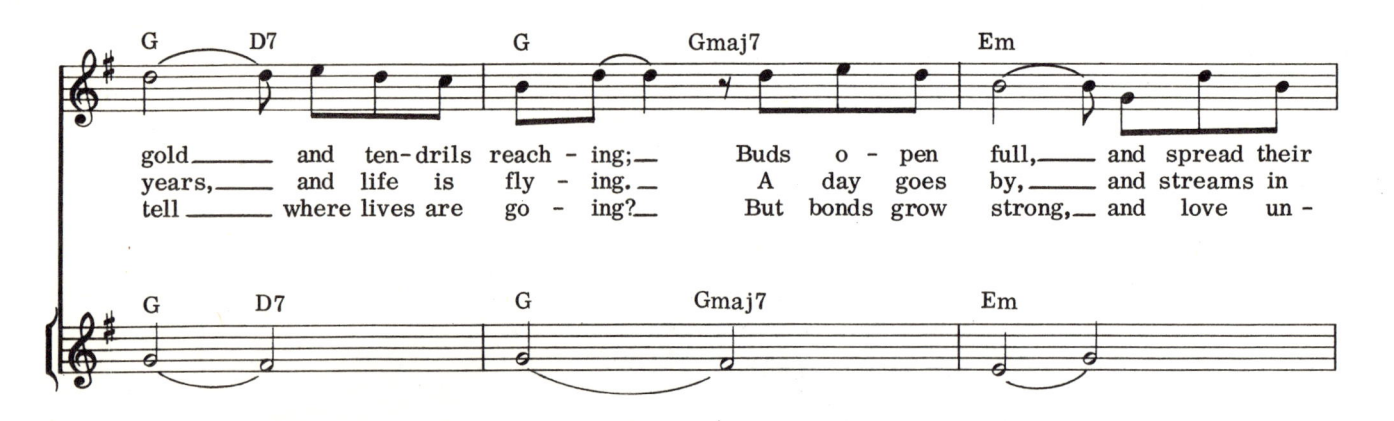

1. Shells fall a-way, and roots take hold, with arch-ing
2. A wed-ding comes, and flows on by, and turns to
3. Friends fall a-way, and mem-'ries fade, and who can

(A few voices, or an instrument) Ooh

gold and ten-drils reach-ing; Buds o-pen full, and spread their
years, and life is fly-ing. A day goes by, and streams in
tell where lives are go-ing? But bonds grow strong, and love un-

wings, and sing the song that time is teach-ing.
time, in joy and love that time is buy-ing.
folds, and har-vests gold from all the sow-ing.

Copyright © 1970 by Nick Hodsdon

Go Watch a Bird

When Margie Colonese and the former Father Jim Fitzgibbon, O.F.M., decided to marry, they chose Matt. 6:25-34 for the Gospel reading at their nuptial Mass. The scripture they chose is lovely, but it's hard. Who can go live like a "bird of the air," for heaven's sake? Who can "go, sell all that you have and give it to the poor," and still be responsible to his own potential and to those who depend on him?

It seems to me that Jesus' point was about anxiety, worrying about saving yourself instead of trusting God—and especially saving yourself by saving up more material goods than you need. (Jesus seems to have had a real thing against storing up stuff; see Matthew 6:19 ff, Matthew 6:26 ff, Luke 12:16 ff, Mark 10:21 ff, etc. He seems to have been particularly anti-barn.) Still, I don't think he **was** telling people to be nonconstructive—an Idle Dandy, Miss Lilly de LaField, a Cow of Bashan—or to flutter irresponsibly through life the way a butterfly might appear to do.

Butterflies and hummingbirds don't go around with long faces, but they are responsible to the flowers they pollinate. The flowers feed them, they put out colors and fragrances to attract them, but the principal thing in a flower's mind is to produce good seed for the next generation of flowers (and correlatively for the next generation of butterflies, and of men). And birds are busy as bees, and beavers work like beavers. But they don't *worry* about it. They seem to do what's good to do, and trust somebody that they have a right to be here. They don't have to prove anything; they seem to enjoy being beautiful, and they sing!

I told Jim and Margie I'd try to set the passage to music, but I just didn't and I didn't and I didn't until the morning of the wedding, when I finally made myself sit down to it (in the bathtub, as a matter of fact), and "Go Watch a Bird" is what came out.

A congregation will catch on to this in no time. After the first verse or so, add the harmony-echo part with a few voices or a flute. Sounds good with lazy three-finger Travis picking. (Note: C/B means a C chord with a B in the bass.)

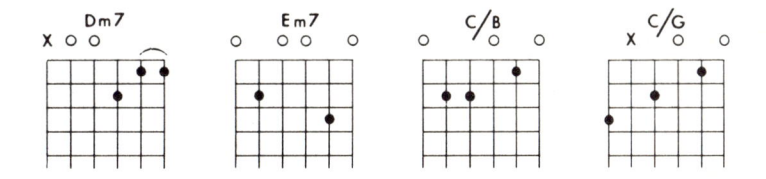

Go Watch a Bird!

For Jim and Margie Fitzgibbon

Matthew 6:25 - 34

Words and music by Nick Hodsdon

Slowly, easily

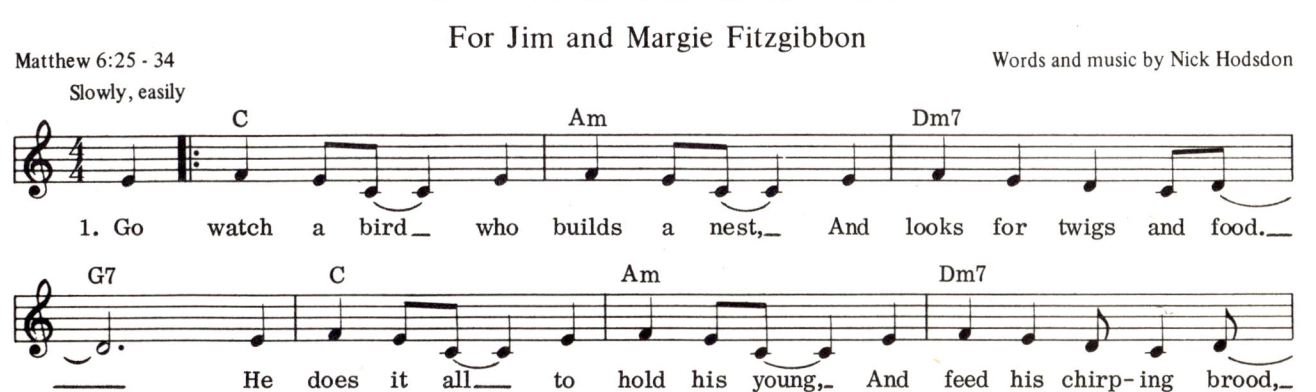

1. Go watch a bird who builds a nest, And looks for twigs and food. He does it all to hold his young, And feed his chirp-ing brood,

2. Go watch a flower. Its colors glow. It sweetens up the breeze,
Calls butterflies and hummingbirds, And all to make a seed;
   That's how it sings! It sings—
   It opens in the sunlight, and it sings.
While flowers grow, birds fill the sky; What worries has a butterfly?

3. For birds to earn their right to live is too inane for words.
They don't put bugs in banks and barns, impressing other birds.
   Instead they sing! They sing—
   They fill the air with music and they sing.
While flowers grow, birds fill the sky; What worries has a butterfly?

4. A flower fills tomorrow's fields by building seeds today,
But if it tried to prove respectability this way,
   It couldn't sing! Not sing—
   Tomorrow's fields are bare if you don't sing.
The flowers die when new days dawn, And so will we when life is gone.
So why not sing? Yes, sing—
Each day is all we're given, so let's sing. . . .

(musical variation for final two lines of song)

58

Father Almighty

Remember that the melody for this one is on the bottom line. It sounds okay if everybody just sings this line in unison, sounds better when somebody adds the top line, better still with full harmony. Add parts according to your resources! Any line can be sung by men or by women—experiment, and see which you like best.

The tune is based on "San Sereni," a children's song from Mexico. It lends itself to a rhythmic treatment (with maracas, etc.) and to a soft, quiet reading; we favor the latter. It can be used as a call to prayer, as a prayer in itself, and as a prayer response. I always get a little twinge in realizing God's patience when I honestly face the reality of the third phrase.

Father Almighty
A Prayer

Words by Nick Hodsdon

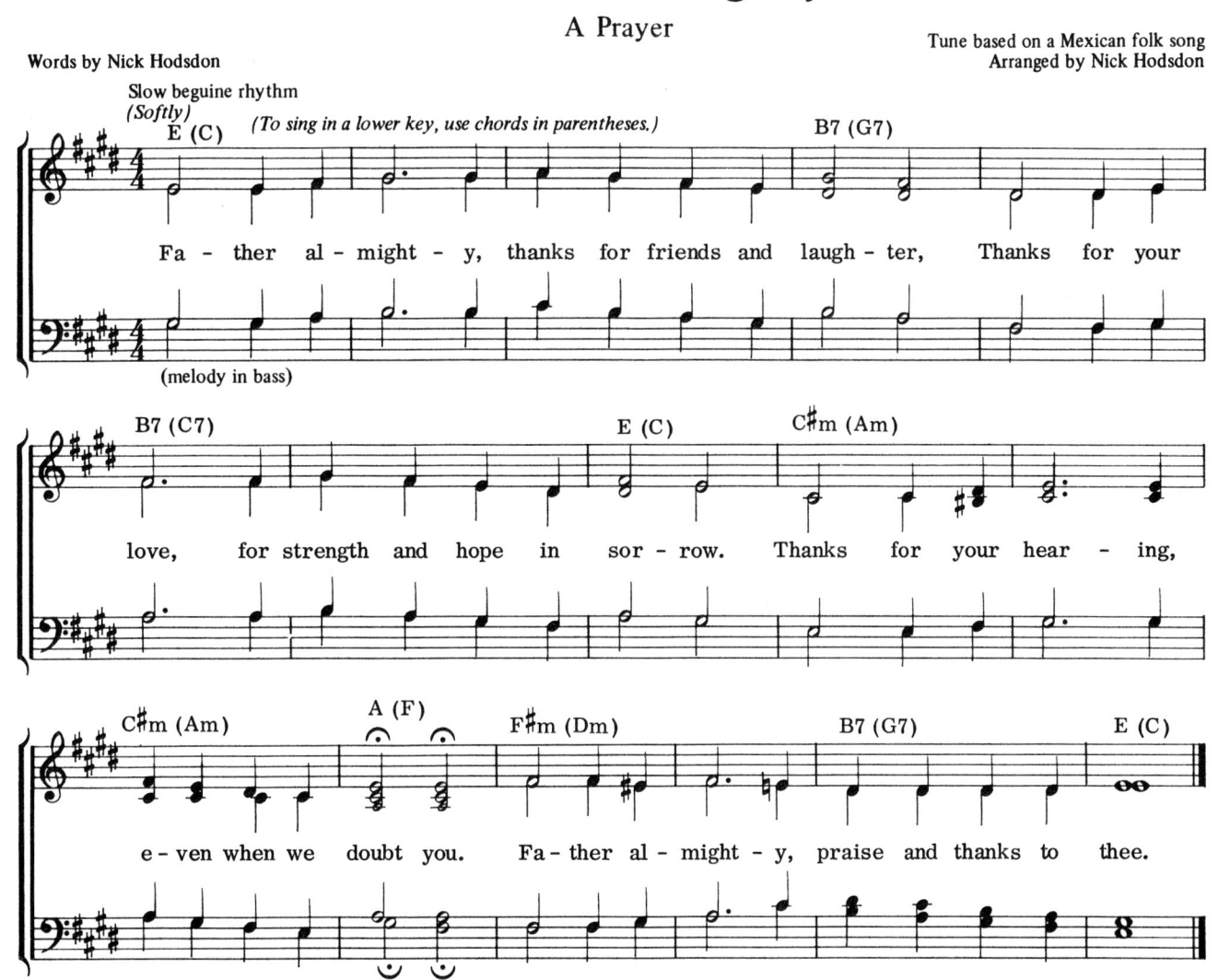

Tune based on a Mexican folk song
Arranged by Nick Hodsdon

Slow beguine rhythm (Softly)
(To sing in a lower key, use chords in parentheses.)
(melody in bass)

Fa-ther al-might-y, thanks for friends and laugh-ter, Thanks for your love, for strength and hope in sor-row. Thanks for your hear-ing, e-ven when we doubt you. Fa-ther al-might-y, praise and thanks to thee.

Copyright © 1970 by Nick Hodsdon

May That Circle Be Unbroken

This is especially good to sing if everybody can come up and make one or two circles of people with the bride and groom around the Communion table—even if it comes to a hundred people or so. They could all stay there together for the Prayer of Thanksgiving, Pronouncement, Dismissal, and whatever, and then follow the wedding party out, at the Recessional. It's a great tune to sing while walking to the table or Communion rail. In fact, one version is still used in the South as a spirited marching hymn for funerals, anticipating the unbroken circle in Eternity. (See *Offertory*, pp. 31-32.)

The words come right from the traditional Consecration Prayers, although here we follow the earliest Christian liturgies in joyfully remembering the living Christ rather than reflecting somberly on his death. Like "On My Journey," this hymn welcomes percussion and spontaneous adding of new verses. No need to make them rhyme.

As with all hymns during which people will be moving, sing at least one verse all the way through before the moving gets started. To give an added spark toward the end of the singing, play a D7 chord and modulate up to the key of G. Then play the chords in parentheses.

May That Circle Be Unbroken
A Communion Hymn

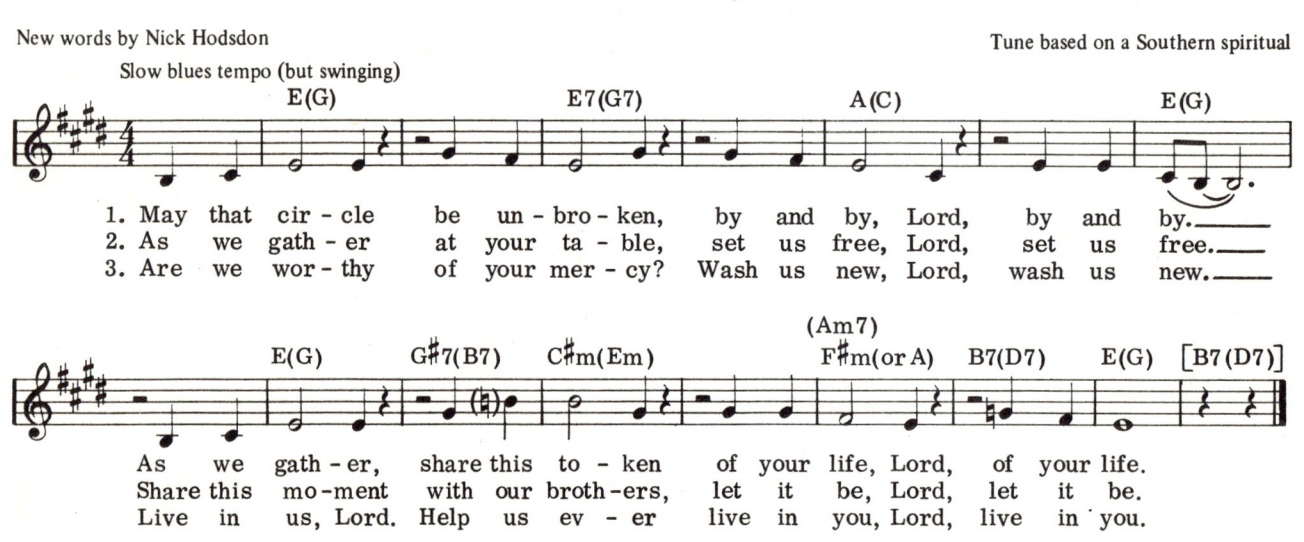

New words by Nick Hodsdon

Tune based on a Southern spiritual

Slow blues tempo (but swinging)

1. May that cir-cle be un-bro-ken, by and by, Lord, by and by.
2. As we gath-er at your ta-ble, set us free, Lord, set us free.
3. Are we wor-thy of your mer-cy? Wash us new, Lord, wash us new.

As we gath-er, share this to-ken of your life, Lord, of your life.
Share this mo-ment with our broth-ers, let it be, Lord, let it be.
Live in us, Lord. Help us ev-er live in you, Lord, live in you.

Copyright © 1970 by Nick Hodsdon

Pax Vobiscum

This is an ancient element of the Mass, probably dating back to its inclusion in the Gospel of John (14:27). It occurs (and can be sung) at various points in liturgies of the historical-sacramental traditions, and can be used as a prayer response or as a closing element in services of the Reformed and Anabaptist traditions. This tune has its roots in a wistful folk song from Vermont called "I Saw the Trace of the Wind in the Trees." Sing it softly, and slowly.

We like to sing it in unison first in the original Latin, and then in parts in English. (It may be the only easy Latin text that most people get to sing anymore; maybe that's why the people in my church like to do this.) It also lets you sing it twice, which is much more pleasing, without getting bored at the repetition of the words.

In the canon of the Mass, this could be sung right after the Greeting of Peace which follows the Lord's Prayer. If people have been moving around shaking hands, the song leader should say something like "Now let us sing the Pax Vobiscum, on page xx."

At the time of Christ people commonly greeted each other with a "kiss of peace," which was incorporated into the Christian services in New Testament times. We like to close services with a form of this; if the worshipers don't quite feel comfortable kissing or hugging one another, we just take the hands of the nearest person and say, "Peace be with you, John." He responds, "And with your spirit, Nick," and then passes the Peace on to the next person. Then we all sing the "Pax Vobiscum."

(See "The Kiss of Peace," p. 26.)

Pax Vobiscum

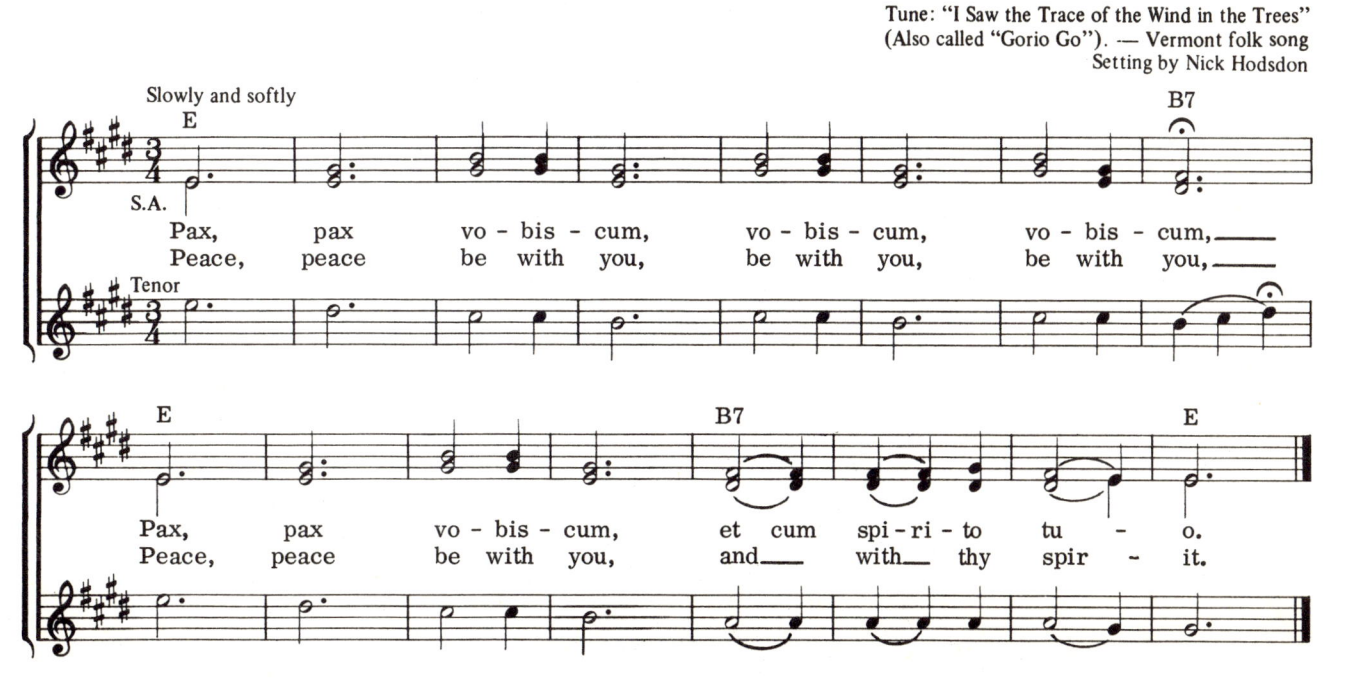

Tune: "I Saw the Trace of the Wind in the Trees"
(Also called "Gorio Go"). — Vermont folk song
Setting by Nick Hodsdon

Slowly and softly

Pax, pax vo-bis-cum, vo-bis-cum, vo-bis-cum,
Peace, peace be with you, be with you, be with you,

Pax, pax vo-bis-cum, et cum spi-ri-to tu-o.
Peace, peace be with you, and with thy spir-it.

Copyright © 1970 by Nick Hodsdon

There's Many a River

This one is really nice. I thought of it as a Communion hymn (I asked Sister Ann Christine what she thought should be in a Eucharist hymn and then made her a song out of the elements she mentioned), but people seem to like to use it for gatherings, partings, ordinations—I didn't understand quite what I had written until it was six months old and we sang it at a joint Catholic-Protestant service, and suddenly I saw that it was about getting together. So I think it's the right song for a wedding.

The tune comes from an old cowboy song about the rivers of Texas. Everybody learns it easily, and it's got plenty of verses, so for traditional Masses you can use it during the long offertory section or for the Communion itself. (See *The Communion Rite*, p. 33, for other ideas.) It's so gentle and persuasive that it makes it easy to get the whole congregation to get up and flow together around the Communion table, like a joining of little streams into the circling Oceanus. There is a river, the waters of which make glad the city of God.

There's Many a River That Waters the Land

A Communion Hymn

Words by Nick Hodsdon

Tune: Traditional
Setting by Nick Hodsdon

Refrain

Glo-ry to God, and now give me your hand; Glo-ry to God, and now give me your hand. Glo-ry to God, and now give me your hand; there's man-y a riv-er that wa-ters the land.

1. From so man-y plac-es we gath-er to-geth-er,— So man-y peo-ple, we don't know each oth-er;— We find our-selves strang-ers, but

long to be broth-ers.— Lord, make it hap-pen.— We reach out to you.

(Harmony lines for the refrain:)

Glo - ry to God, and now give me your hand; Glo - ry to God and now give me your hand. Glo - ry to God, and now give me your hand; there's man-y— a riv-er— that wa-ters— the land.

2. So many distances, so many journeys,
   So many chasms and so many turnings,
   So many bridges just now are a-building.
   Lord, make it happen. We reach out to you.

3. From songs still silent, and eyes to be opened,
   Dreams newly borning, and love still unspoken,
   Dreaming so different, still love can awaken.
   Lord, make it happen. We reach out to you.

4. In bread and in wine, and in tears and in laughter,
   So many roads in the parting soon after,
   Handclasp and teasing, refreshing and feeding.
   Lord, make it happen. We reach out to you.

5. Sharing together the food for the journey,
   River of wine, in our lives cool and burning,
   Sharing the faith of the bread new-sustaining.
   Lord, make it happen. We reach out to you.

6. Here at the river, both stranger and brother;
   River to distances, turning and dreaming,
   River of ages, of light shared and streaming.
   Lord, make it happen. We reach out to you.

63

The Canon of the Mass

I've encountered many many folk-style settings of the ordinaries of the Mass (i.e., the parts that are ordinarily done at every complete service), but I've found very few thoroughly good ones. The problem may have been the composer's compulsion to come up with something, no matter how strained, for all the major parts (the Kyrie, the Gloria, the Credo, the Sanctus, the Lord's Prayer, and the Agnus Dei). The Gloria and the Credo feel absolutely interminable in most of these versions—there are just so many words to plow through.

At the big Roman Catholic church at which my guitar and I lead a Mass every week, we've tried a simpler approach: we just go ahead and say the longer parts of the Mass and sing instead the shorter ones that are usually spoken, and we've concentrated on developing music for the canon of the Mass (see outline on pp. 35-36). We've come up with a set of short, simple musical elements that work well week after week. You'll find melody lines for the congregational singing of all these all together on the "canon sheets" (beginning below), with the Lord's Prayer on pp. 66-67, ready to be duplicated for your own wedding congregation; and you'll find harmonizations and suggestions on how to use them on the following pages. (The commentary on the "Pax Vobiscum" is on page 61.)

During the canon of the Mass, it will be awkward to interrupt the prayers in order to tell people when to sing, so just before the Sursum Corda ("Lift up your hearts . . .") the priest could tell people that the music for the next five songs will be found on the "canon sheet" (which could be a different color for easy location), and that they are invited to find these songs and sing along. Then, as the songs come up, the priest could just say, for example, "Now let us sing the Memorial Acclamation" instead of saying his usual words, "Let us proclaim the mystery of faith." The word "sing" and a few guitar chords should be all the direction people will need in order to join in, if the music has been sung once, before the service.

The Canon of the Mass

The Sanctus

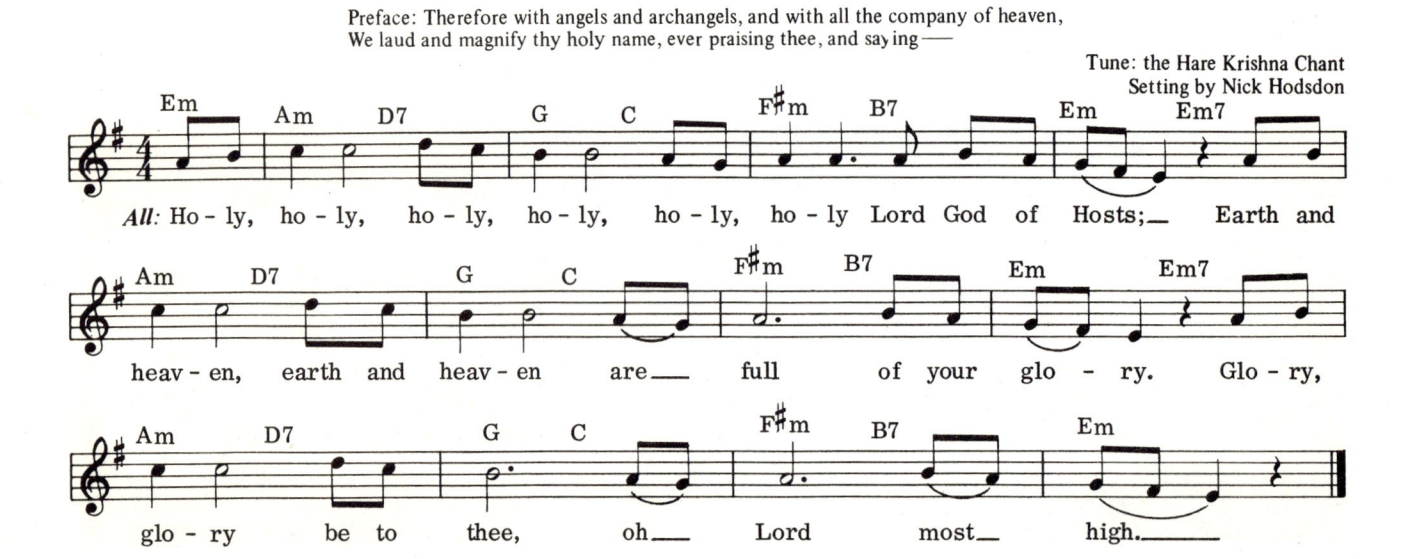

Preface: Therefore with angels and archangels, and with all the company of heaven,
We laud and magnify thy holy name, ever praising thee, and saying—

Tune: the Hare Krishna Chant
Setting by Nick Hodsdon

All: Ho-ly, ho-ly, ho-ly, ho-ly, ho-ly, ho-ly Lord God of Hosts;— Earth and heav-en, earth and heav-en are— full of your glo-ry. Glo-ry, glo-ry be to thee, oh— Lord most— high.

The Benedictus

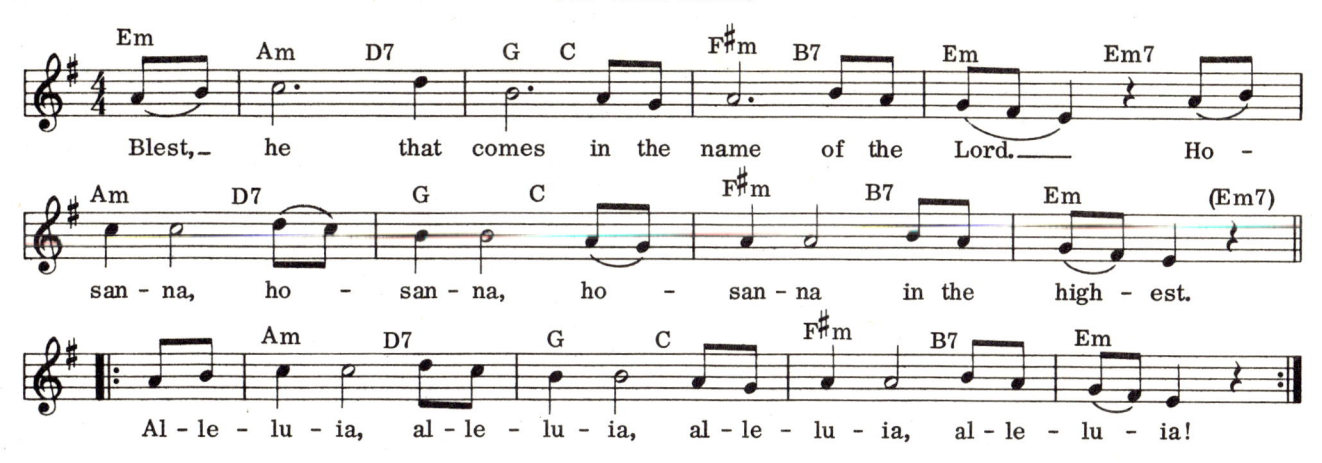

Blest, he that comes in the name of the Lord. Ho-sanna, ho-sanna, ho-sanna in the high-est.

Al-le-lu-ia, al-le-lu-ia, al-le-lu-ia, al-le-lu-ia!

The Memorial Acclamation

Tune and setting by Nick Hodsdon

All: Christ has died; Christ is ris-en;— Christ will come a-gain; Christ will come a-gain.

The Great Amen

Based on Karg-Elert's "Triumphal March"
Tune and setting by Nick Hodsdon

A-men, a-men, al-le-lu-ia, a-men, Al-le-lu-ia, al-le-lu-ia, al-le-lu-ia, a-men!

The Lord's Prayer

(on the back of this page)

The Pax Vobiscum

Tune: "Gorio Go," a Vermont folksong
Setting by Nick Hodsdon

Pax, pax vo-bis-cum, vo-bis-cum, vo-bis-cum;
Peace, peace be with you, be with you, be with you;

Pax, pax vo-bis-cum, Et cum spi-ri-tu tu-o.
Peace, peace be with you, and— with— thy spir-it.

65

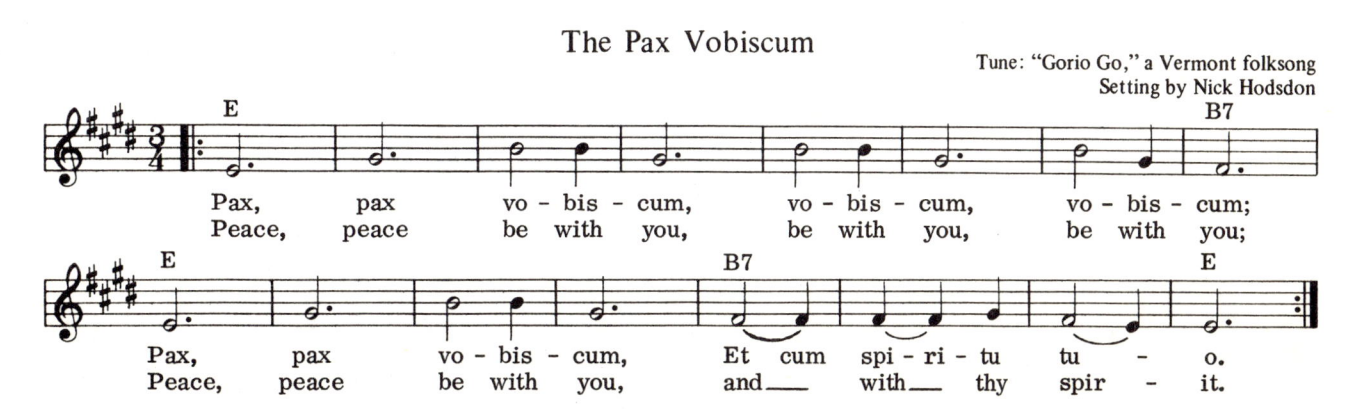

The Lord's Prayer

This is the one element of the service that all the worshipers will probably know, and in which they could all join easily, so you may want to keep this as a spoken prayer.

But sometimes things can become so familiar that they're hard to think about. The refreshing quality of music can take the meanings within familiar words and make them available again. So we usually like to have the congregation sing the Lord's Prayer together.

There are a number of good folk-style settings of this prayer available. Here is a new one based on an old English folk song. When this tune appeared as a seventeenth-century broadside ballad, the original words were "Tomorrow shall be my dancing day . . ." An activity as happy as praying should retain the grace and the liveliness and the happiness of the dance. Sing this one slowly, but with a gentle lilt.

Guitarists: Am, Bm, and plain C sound almost as good as Am7, Bm7, and Cmaj7. If you're not yet up to a Bm or a Bm7, substitute an Em7 instead. It's an incredibly easy chord, but it's very rich.

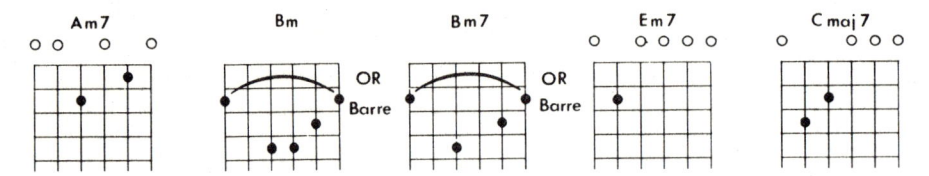

Also: If there's nobody around who can play the three instrumental interludes, just strum the indicated chords (or a reasonable facsimile thereof).

The Lord's Prayer

Tune based on a traditional English ballad
Setting by Nick Hodsdon

Our Fa-ther who art in heav-en, Hal-low-ed be thy name. Thy king-dom come. Thy will be done, on earth as it is in heav-en. The king-dom is thine, the pow-er is thine, the glo-ry thine, for-ev-er, for-

Copyright © 1970 by Nick Hodsdon

Am D7 G G Em Am7 D7G G Am7 Bm7 Am7
ev - er. (instrumental) Our Fa-ther who art in heav - en,
G C Am D7 Bm C Am7 D7
Give us this day our dai - ly bread, and for-give us our debts, for-give us our debts, as
and for - give us all our tres - pass - es, as
G Em Am7 D7 G C D
we for - give our debt - ors.
we for-give those who tres - pass a - gainst us. The king - dom is thine, the
Bm (rit.) C Em Am Cmaj7 D D7 G Em Am7 D7 G
pow - er is thine, the glo - ry thine, for - ev - er, for - ev - er. (instru-mental)
Em Am7 D7 G G Am7 Bm7 Am7
(instrumental) Our Fa-ther who art in heav - en,
G C Am D Bm C Am7 D7
Lead us not in - to temp - ta - tion, but de - liv - er us from e - vil, for
G Em Am7 D7 G C D Bm C (rit.) Em
thine is the king-dom, the glo - ry and power. The king-dom is thine, the pow-er is thine, the
Am Cmaj7 D (a tempo) D7 G Em Am D7 G G Em Am7 D7 G
glo - ry thine, for - ev - er, for - ev - er! (instrumental)

Sanctus and Benedictus

I've been told that the tune to this one may be over a thousand years old, although you may have first heard it as the music for the "Be In" scene from the Broadway musical *Hair*. The music is hypnotic, and you can lose yourself in using it to sing God's praises over and over. Once you get to know this melody, you'll understand why it's lasted so long!

The words of the Sanctus don't try to teach or preach; they don't petition for anything; they just sort of stand there and say "Wow!" What a treasure we've been given—the liberty to stand before God and sing to him! To say "Alleluia, praise you, glory to you, Holy Lord."

Whatever the Proper Preface that precedes the Sanctus, it will always end with some formula saying that we are going to join all the choirs of angels in heaven in singing their unending hymn of praise, the Sanctus. (The word "angels" can be the musicians' cue to start strumming the chord progressions of the song.) The priest could say the Preface in whatever the prescribed form, and then a singer could reiterate it with the words on p. 68 ("Therefore, with angels . . .") as a lead-in to the Sanctus. It uses the same melody as the Sanctus, and a congregation will sail into the "Holy, Holy" with greater verve and confidence after hearing the tune sung to them in the Preface. If you wish, the Sanctus could lead, *verso segue*, into the Benedictus.

Once the Sanctus is established, encourage people to make up harmony lines, using the simple harmonization here as a starting point. The tune invites embellishment, and almost anything will sound right (except for the F#m measures, where some people's harmonies may clash. If this happens, substitute Am for F#m; it's less beautiful, but it's safer). Once people have gotten into it you may want to go back to the "Holy, Holy" verse and sing it all again, or repeat the "Alleluia" verse several times. It's nice to end it quietly by having an instrument (flute, xylophone, etc.) play the melody one final time while the guitars strum and one or two voices hum a harmony line.

Sanctus and Benedictus

Tune: Hare Krishna chant
Setting by Nick Hodsdon

Preface

(Leader only) There-fore with an-gels and arch-an-gels, and with all the com-pa-ny of heav-en, We laud and mag-ni-fy thy ho-ly name,_____ ev-er prais-ing thee, and___ say-ing,

Em7 Am D7 G C F♯m B7
(All) Ho - ly ho - ly, ho - ly ho - ly, ho - ly ho - ly, Lord God of
Alto
Em Em7 Am D7 G C F♯m B7
Hosts. Earth and heav - en, earth and heav - en are full of your
Ah
Em Em7 Am D7 G C F♯m B7 Em Em7
glo - ry. Glo - ry, glo - ry be to thee, oh Lord Most High.
Ah
(optional Benedictus)
Am D7 G C F♯m B7 Em Em7
Blest, he that comes in the name of the Lord. Ho -
Ah
Am D7 G C F♯m B7 Em Em7
san - na, ho - san - na, ho - san - na in the high - est.
Ah
Am D7 G C F♯m B7 Em
repeat ad lib.
Al - le - lu - ia, al - le - lu - ia, al - le - lu - ia, al - le - lu - ia!
Al - le - lu, al - le - lu, al - le - lu - ia!

Memorial Acclamation

This is the briefest of the four Memorial Acclamations. The priest will have just completed the part of the Eucharistic Prayer which describes the Lord's Supper, ending with the words of Jesus: "Take this, all of you, and drink from it: this is the cup of my blood, the blood of the new and everlasting covenant. It will be shed for you and for all men so that sins may be forgiven. Do this in memory of me." He will then say "Let us proclaim the mystery of faith," or "Let us sing the Memorial Acclamation."

Play a D and then an A7 chord, and people should join right in. Sing it once in unison, then play an A7 and do it again with some women's voices doing the "echo" on the second part. If there are already some built-in echoes in the church, the texture might get a little thick if you have voices singing the third part too, so you might try having one of your instruments play it instead.

Memorial Acclamation

Setting by Nick Hodsdon

The Great Amen

    This comes at the liturgical climax of the Eucharist, immediately after the bread and wine have been consecrated. The cue is the priest's concluding doxology: "Through him, with him, in him, in the unity of the Holy Spirit, all glory and honor is yours, almighty Father, forever and ever." Be ready with a few chords to start it off. It should be a rousing assent to God's gift of life.

    The melody is very easy to pick up; the harmony is a lot of fun to do, but the bass line is a little tricky (especially the jump from the third "Amen" to the next "Alleluia"—fair warning, basses!). Again, anybody can sing any part at any octave (so I should say, "Fair warning, anybody who decides to sing the bottom line"). One choir director put his high sopranos on the middle line, one octave higher. The result was quite startling...

    A week or so after I wrote this, it began to sound awfully familiar, and then I realized that I had borrowed it from a triumphal march by the nineteenth-century German organist Sigfrid Karg-Elert, who had borrowed it from a seventeenth-century chorale called "Nun Danket" by Johann Crüger, and we're not quite sure where Crüger got it from.

The Great Amen

Based on a theme from "Triumphal March" by Karg-Elert
Setting by Nick Hodsdon

On My Journey

A text for the bride's mother! And now is the time for the full joy of the day to break out. Now is the time to tap your percussion resources—to tap on things, jingle things, bang things together. Now is the time to coax the congregation into the aisles, to march with the bride and groom on their journey to the next phase of their life together, and to the fellowship that extends the worship service.

Instruments and song leaders should stay close together, and should stay behind most of the recessing congregation so that everybody can hear them and stay together in rhythm. If you get to the end of the song and there's still lots of recessing to do, just start over again. Or, better yet, make up some verses on the spot. Since each verse has only a single line, there's nothing to rhyme. Any single line in trochaic heptameter will do (and it's much easier to write a trochaic heptameter than it is to define one).

For the last few verses, modulate up to the key of G and listen to the voices swell! You might even want to gather at the back of the church and sing "He's Got the Whole World in His Hands," or "Amen." While you're at it, do "Joy Is Now" again. And then "There's Many a River." And then . . .

Guitarists: If you can't find G#m7 and/or F#m fast enough, just leave one or both of them out and go to B7 on "weep."

To transpose to G, follow the chords in parentheses.

On My Journey

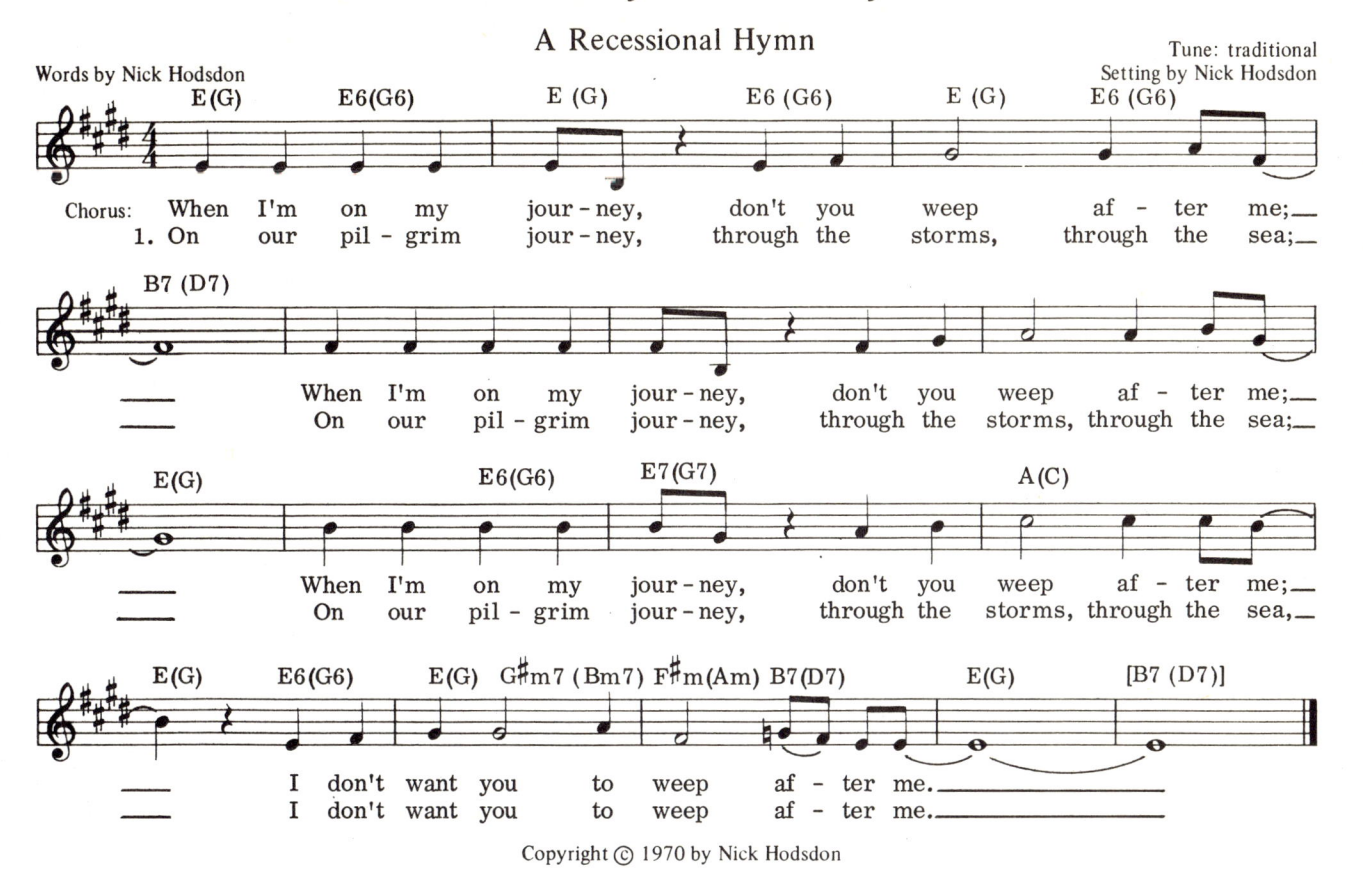

A Recessional Hymn

Words by Nick Hodsdon

Tune: traditional
Setting by Nick Hodsdon

Chorus:
When I'm on my jour-ney, don't you weep af-ter me;
When I'm on my jour-ney, don't you weep af-ter me;
When I'm on my jour-ney, don't you weep af-ter me;
I don't want you to weep af-ter me.

1. On our pil-grim jour-ney, through the storms, through the sea;
On our pil-grim jour-ney, through the storms, through the sea;
On our pil-grim jour-ney, through the storms, through the sea,
I don't want you to weep af-ter me.

Copyright © 1970 by Nick Hodsdon

2. Standing close together, face the world joyfully, (*sing three times*)
I don't want you to weep after me.

3. Trials and tribulations still that none can foresee; (*sing three times*)
I don't want you to weep after me.

4. Out into the vineyard, harvest gold finally. (*sing three times*)
I don't want you to weep after me.

5. Joy and tears and laughter, let it come, let it be; (*sing three times*)
I don't want you to weep after me.

(*If you're going right on to a reception, add the following*):

6. As we go together, come and break bread with me; (*sing three times*)
I don't want you to weep after me.

IV. ONE VERSION OF HOW THIS COULD ALL FIT TOGETHER

Songs of Welcome and Fellowship and Celebration (while greeting the guests): "Go Watch a Bird," etc.

Call to Worship (Jeremiah 33:10b-11)

Entrance of the bride and groom, down opposite aisles from the back of the church, etc. (Song of Solomon 8:13, 14; Psalm 68:24-26) Processional Hymn: "Joy Is Now"

Greeting and *Preparation*: instead of saying why they should not be joined together, have someone say why they should be. Proof text: Ecclesiastes 4:7-12.
    Response: "The Raddle of Love"

Charge to the Couple
    Epistle: Genesis 2:4b-7, 18-24; then Genesis 1:27-31a
    Gradual: "Love Is a Double Helix," verses 1 and 2, with refrain
    Gospel: Matthew 19:4-6
    Response: "Love Is a Double Helix," verse 3, final refrain and coda

Leave-taking (Mark 10:6-7)
    Response: "Sunrise, Sunset"

Meditations and Reflections on Marriage (homily; shared reflections; interpretations through film, dance, and dialogue)

Promises and Vows, or alternative readings by the bride and groom
    Response: "Love Is a Double Helix," final refrain and coda

Giving and Receiving of Rings; Blessing of Rings
    Response: "Unfolding"

Responsory, Litany, or *Responsive Reading,* calling the congregation to prayer
    Response: "Father Almighty"

Call to Confession, Confession, and *Assurance of Pardon*
    Response and Hymn of Fellowship: "Pax Vobiscum" segueing into "Man Is the Joy of Man"

Offertory and the gathering at the table. Hymn: "May That Circle Be Unbroken"

The *"Lord's Prayer,"* and *Communion*. Communion Hymn: "There's Many a River"

Prayers of Blessing, Pronouncement-Affirmation, with balloons. (Ecclesiastes 9:9)

Recessional (Song of Solomon 7:11-12). Hymn: "On My Journey"

Other Ideas

Have a candlelight wedding.

Have the reception first; begin the "Solemnization of Matrimony" after the guests have gotten to know and to like one another and have become a family.

Hire a high-school chorus to sing the wedding music from *Lohengrin*.

Elope.

Planning List for Designing Your Wedding

A basic verity to keep in mind: *The more places you plan to use music, the better it'll be!*

1. *Wedding invitations:* Any particular colors, and/or visual symbols (butterfly, dove, joined hands), to be used again throughout the wedding as a motif in banners, program, clothes, reception accouterments? _____.
Any suggestions for the guests regarding dress? ("Everybody wear yellow"; "Jeans and bare feet for all"; "Brightest colors possible") _____.
An invitation (maybe issued only to special friends) to prepare and share thoughts, poems, songs, during offertory or homily or reception? _____.
Who would you ask? _____.

2. What sort of *visual environment* do you want *outside* the gathering place? _____. Who would help fix it up? _____.

3. What sort of *visuals* do you want *inside*? _____. Who could help? _____.

4. Where can you get *flowers*? _____. Fabrics for banners? _____. Other visuals and *environment makers?* (bells, wind chimes, balloons, bubble stuff, records of birdsong) _____. Who could help? _____.

5. What *style of dress* for bride and groom, bridesmaids, etc.? _____.

6. Any special *vestments* for the clergy? Who could make them? _____.

7. Who will *welcome* and seat guests? (bride and groom? groomsmen? family?) _____.
What will you give everybody to get them in the mood? (a daisy? a balloon? a lavalier bell? a banana?) _____.

8. What *sounds and songs* will be going on as people come in? (birds singing; bells ringing; familiar songs and spirituals) _____.

9. Sketch the *ground plan* of the room, area, or church. Sketch in the way you'd like to arrange people—bride, groom, singers, priests, prie-dieus, mothers, Communion tables, friends and neighbors—during different parts of the service. (Use a pencil; you'll probably change your mind.)

10. What would you like for an *invocation* and a *scriptural summoning* of the bride, the groom, the wedding procession? _____.
Who will read these? (minister? parents? song leader? bride and groom?) _____.

11. How will you work the *processional?* What will you sing? _____.
Who will be in the bride's group? _____.
In the groom's? _____.
Sketch out where they'll enter, where they'll go, where they'll meet.

12. What will your *Greeting, Preparation, and Charge to the Couple* be? (Also see the marriage rite of your own denomination.) _____.
Will you have a song here, or perhaps another verse of a song sung earlier? _____.

13. If the wedding isn't part of a traditional Mass, would you like to have some inspirational readings or *scripture readings* here? _____.
Who will read them? _____.

THE JOYFUL WEDDING

  From where? _____
  What songs would illuminate the readings? _____.
14. Who would you like to have give some words of *meditation*?
  Old couple _____ Young couple _____.
  Family friends _____ Minister _____.
  Who could prepare a homily-meditation through film? _____.
  Through music? _____ Through dance? _____.
  Is there another song, or a verse of a song sung earlier, that would illuminate some of the meditations or would be a meditation in itself? _____
15. Who should be involved in a *leave-taking circle dance*? _____.
  Who should be involved in a *leave-taking ceremony*? _____.
  Sketch out who would be where before, during, and after.
  What should be sung or played to illuminate leave-taking? _____.
16. Will you have an *Introduction to the Vows*? _____.
17. What basic pledges do you want your *Promises* and *Vows* to cover? What do you think you'd want to be held to, five years from now? _____
_____
_____

  On a separate sheet, sketch out sample promises and/or vows for the bride and for the groom.
  What would be the best songs for this most important moment? _____.
  The music could function like the bread in a club sandwich. What verses could you sing where? Before the vows: _____.
  After the bride's vows: _____.
  After the groom's: _____.
  Who'll sing it? (whole congregation? a soloist?) _____.
18. Who will introduce or bless the *rings*? _____.
  With what words? _____
_____

  What will you say in giving the rings to each other? _____
_____
_____

  Will you have the ceremony of the *sweet and bitter wines*? _____.
  Who will introduce this? (minister? parents? friends?) _____.
  What should be sung? _____.
  Would you sing different verses after the bride's words? _____.
  The groom's words? _____. The wine ritual? ____
_____. Who will sing it? (whole congregation? a soloist?) _____.
19. Would you prefer a *pronouncement* by the minister or an *affirmation* by the congregation? _____. Who should say the scriptural response? _____.
  What song for this happy moment? _____. What physical sign of happiness? (Everybody ring bells? blow soap bubbles? throw balloons? drink a toast? kiss the bride? kiss the groom?) _____

A. IF WEDDING IS NOT TO BE PART OF A SERVICE OF HOLY COMMUNION:
20. Who would say which *nuptial blessing*? (minister? parents? friends?) _____.
  What would you sing? _____.

PLANNING LIST FOR DESIGNING YOUR WEDDING

21. Would you like to pray the *Lord's Prayer?* _____. In spoken word or song? _____
22. Will you exchange the *Kiss of Peace?* _____. Who will initiate it? _____.
    With what words? _____
    What will the "receiver" say in response? _____.
    Sketch the path the initial passers should take.
    Should people be stationary, or circulating and congratulating? _____.
    What music, once the Peace has gotten started? _____.
    Conclude with "Pax Vobiscum" all together?
23. What should the minister (or family or friends) say in *benediction?* _____
    _____
    _____
    _____

    What should the bride and groom say? _____
    _____
24. Who will follow whom in the *recessional?* Where will you go to? _____
    _____
    What music? _____. What instruments could be passed out?
    (tambourines; washboard; spoons; bells; kazoos; bangable pans) _____.
    What will you throw at the bride and groom? (flowers? bubbles? congratulations?) _____
    _____.

B. IF THE WEDDING IS TO INCLUDE A SERVICE OF THE LORD'S SUPPER OR AN AGAPE FEAST, this could occur at the very beginning, right after the *processional* or the *greeting* (Planning List #11 & 12), or after the *blessing and giving of rings* (#18), or after the *affirmation and pronouncement* (#19). Where would you place it? _____.

For an Agape Feast, what words of invitation would be used? Who would say them? _____
_____
_____

What would you sing? _____.
The Service of the Lord's Supper could follow immediately from an Agape Feast of fruit and nuts and cheese. What words would you use to distinguish this period as Holy Communion, before the prayers of consecration? _____.

Who would read this? _____. Would you want to sing one more verse of the Agape song above? _____
To conclude the service, see planning list #20-24 under A.

C. IF THE WEDDING IS SIMPLY TO BE CONCLUDED, AFTER STEP #19, WITH A CELEBRATION OF THE LORD'S SUPPER, follow with:

20. *Nuptial Blessings* (see #20 under A)
21. *Lord's Prayer* (see #21 under A)
22. *Confession and Assurance of Pardon* (p. 28). Would you prefer this earlier in the service (e.g. after the *Greeting,* before the *Preparation* and *Charge to the Couple,* step #12)?_____
    What will you read for a Call to Confession? _____
    Who could read it? (minister, song leader, parents, etc.) _____.
    What response would the congregation make? _____
    What music in response? _____. Will there be an Assurance of Pardon? Who will say it? (minister? everybody?) What words? _____
    _____.
23. *Kiss of Peace* (see #22 under A)

THE JOYFUL WEDDING

24. At the *offertory*, who will bring forward the bread and wine? _____.
Who could bake the bread? _____. Will there be a collection of money offerings for the church? _____. Who will collect it? _____.
Sketch out the route by which the congregation will gather around the Communion table. Who will lead them? _____. What may have to be moved? (chairs, prie-dieus, music stands) _____.
Who will move it? _____ What song for the gathering together? _____.

Once gathered, will you include an offering of the gifts of wisdom and of continuing love and support? _____. Who should introduce this and explain it? _____.
Who would you like to mention it to beforehand? (best friends? close relatives? etc.) _____.

25. At *Communion*, who will distribute the bread? The wine? (the bride and groom? the minister? the congregation, from hand to hand?) _____.
Should the minister take the elements around the circle to those who step forward to receive? If you prefer that the congregation receive Communion one by one at the altar, sketch out the route by which those receiving will get there and how they will get back to the table. Who will direct traffic? _____.
What should be sung? _____.

26. *Benediction* (see #23 under A)
27. *Recessional* (see #24 under A)

D. IF THE WEDDING IS PART OF A STANDARD NUPTIAL MASS, Roman Catholic or Protestant:
Follow planning steps #1-11, then follow the outline on pp. 34-36.
For section II (*The Service of the Word of God*), see planning steps #13 & 14.
For section IV (*The Rite of Marriage*), see planning steps #12 and #15-19.
For section V (*The Confession of Sin*), see planning step #22 under C.
For section VI (*The Service of the Lord's Supper*), see planning steps #24-25 under C.
(Musical settings of the *Sanctus and Benedictus* will be found on p. 68; of the *Memorial Acclamation*, on p. 70; of the *Great Amen*, on p. 71; of the *Lord's Prayer*, on p. 66).
(For *The Greeting of Peace*, see planning step #22 under A.)
For section VII (*The Concluding Rite*), see planning steps #23-24 under A.

NOW, FOR THE REHEARSAL (OR OTHER PRE-WEDDING GET-TOGETHER): According to what you have decided to include in the list above, what should be practiced? (e.g. the Kiss of Peace, the Affirmation, etc.) _____.

What should be read? (Give readers a chance to try out scriptures and other readings in front of friends.) _____.
What should be sung? _____.

_____ (Sing a lot!)

Final Check List

1. Invitation: colors & symbols _____
   Dress of guests _____ —Who'll share what? _____
2. Outside environment _____ —Who'll help? _____

FINAL CHECK LIST

3. Inside visuals _____ Who'll help? _____
4. Flowers _____ Fabrics _____
   Environment creators _____ Who'll help? _____
5. Bridal party's dress _____
6. Special vestments _____ Who'll make? _____
7. Welcomers _____ Mood-making tokens _____
8. Welcoming sounds _____ Songs _____
9. Floor plan, with people:
10. Invocation/scriptural summoning: words found where? _____
    Who'll read? _____
11. Processional song _____ Bride's group _____
    Groom's group _____ Routing _____
12. Greeting, preparation, charge: words found where? _____
    Song _____
13. Inspirational readings _____ Scripture readings _____
    Who'll read? _____ From what spots? _____
    Song(s) _____
14. Spoken meditations by _____
    Meditations through other media by _____
    Meditation song(s) _____
15. People in leave-taking circle dance _____
    People in leave-taking ceremony _____
    Words found where? _____ Song(s) _____
    What verses where? _____
    Who'll sing? _____
16. Introduction to the vows: found where? _____
17. Vows: found where? _____ Song _____
    What verses where? _____ Who'll sing? _____
18. Who'll introduce/bless rings? _____ Words found where? _____
    Giving/receiving rings: words found where? _____
    Sweet/bitter wine: who'll introduce? _____
    Words found where? _____ Song _____
    What verses where? _____ Who'll sing? _____
19. Pronouncement or affirmation? Who'll give it? _____
    Words found where? _____ Who'll say scriptural response? _____
    Found where? _____ Song _____
    Demonstration _____

A. IF NO COMMUNION:
20. Who gives nuptial blessing? _____
    Words found where? _____ Song _____
21. Lord's Prayer: spoken or sung? _____
22. Kiss of peace: who starts it? _____
    What words? _____
    What path? _____ Guests stationary or circulating? _____
    Music during peace _____ After peace _____
23. Benediction: who gives? _____
    Words found where? _____ Couple's response found where? _____
24. Recessional: What order? _____
    Where to? _____ Song _____
    Instruments for guests _____ Demonstration _____

THE JOYFUL WEDDING

B. AGAPE FEAST:
    Where in service? _____
    Who'll introduce? _____ Words found where? _____
    Song _____ Food _____
    If Holy Communion follows, who'll introduce? _____
    Words found where? _____ Song _____
    (Continue with #20-24 above)

C. LORD'S SUPPER ALONE, AFTER MARRIAGE RITE:
    Nuptial blessing and Lord's Prayer: see #20-21 above.
22. Confession: where in service? _____
    Call: who'll read? _____ Words found where? _____
    Response: words found where? _____ Song _____
    Who'll give Assurance of Pardon? _____
    Words found where? _____
23. Kiss of peace: see A-22.
24. Offertory: Who'll bake it? Who'll bring it to table? _____
    Who'll collect money? _____ Who'll bring guests to table? _____
    Who'll move what out of the way? _____
    Song _____ Who'll introduce "gifts of wisdom and support"? _____ Who's to be told earlier? _____
25. Who'll pass Communion elements? _____
    Who'll direct communicants where? _____
    Song _____ What verses when? _____
26. Benediction: see A-23.
27. Recessional: see A-24.

AT PRE-WEDDING PARTY: Rehearse _____
    Read _____ Sing _____

Copying any of these words or this music by any method, without the author's permission in writing, is a punishable violation of copyright law; but these songs *should* be copied out and given to the congregation, or shared with friends. In addition, those of us who write this sort of thing need feedback! I'd love to know who's using my music and how and why, how they like it, and how I can improve it. So if you want to copy anything in this book, or if you have any suggestions, please write to me at 334 E. 105th Street, #10, New York, N.Y. 10029.

Thanks

Nick Hodsdon